D1190505

CASING
A
PROMISED
LAND

The Autobiography of an Organizational Detective as Cultural Ethnographer

H . L . GOODALL , JR .

Southern Illinois University Press   Carbondale and Edwardsville

Library of Congress Cataloging-in-Publication Data

Goodall, H. Lloyd.
    Casing a promised land : the autobiography of an organizational
detective as cultural ethnographer / H.L. Goodall, Jr.
        p.   cm.
    Bibliography: p.
    ISBN 0-8093-1512-2
    1. Organizational behavior.   2. Corporate culture.
3. Communication in organizations.   I. Title.
HD58.7.G656   1989
302.3'5—dc19   88-39544
                                                    CIP

Written for the Bear, and because of her

with special thanks to

Barry Hannah

Candy and Bill Davis

the participants in the 1986 and 1987 Alta Conference
on Interpretive Approaches to Organizational
Communication

Sandra Bray Sanford

the students in CM 440: Field Study at the University
of Alabama in Huntsville

Susan Gill

Gerald M. Phillips

We in cities rightly grow shrewd at appraising man-made institutions—but beyond these tiny concentration points of rhetoric and traffic, there lies the eternally unsolvable Enigma, the preposterous fact that both existence and nothingness are equally unthinkable. Our speculations may run the whole qualitative gamut, from play, through reverence, even to an occasional shiver of cold metaphysical dread—for always the Eternal Enigma is there, right on the edges of our metropolitan bickerings, stretching outward to interstellar infinity and inward to the depths of the mind. And in this staggering disproportion between man and no-man, there is no place for purely human boasts of grandeur, or for forgetting that men build their cultures by huddling together, nervously loquacious, at the edge of an abyss.

—Kenneth Burke, *Permanence and Change*

Doing ethnography is like trying to read (in the sense of "construct a reading of") a manuscript—foreign, faded, full of ellipses, incoherencies, suspicious emendations, and tendentious commentaries, but written not in conventionalized graphs of sound but in transient examples of shaped behavior.

—Clifford Geertz, *The Interpretation of Cultures*

Contents

What I Do and Why I Do It:
Reading Myself Into the Stories of
Others

Neither the scientific illusion of reality nor the religious reality of
illusion is congruent with the reality of fantasy in the fantasy reality
of the postmodern world. Postmodern ethnography captures this
mood of the postmodern world, for it too does not move toward
abstraction, away from life, but back to experience.

—Stephen A. Tyler, *The Unspeakable*

Because you have to be honest. You are packed
with your past and there is no future.

—Barry Hannah, *Hey Jack!*

Casing a Promised Land is about what happens when an ordinary
scholar of organizational communication decides to get out of the office
and confront a crisis of interpretation.

It is about what happens when he applies the postmodern interpretive
stance he has advanced in lectures, and defended with colleagues, to the
local community where working people manage to survive well enough
without him (and will undoubtedly continue to do so). And it is about
what he finds there as a result of doing just that.

While this statement of motive is true, it may make it seem as if I'd
never been out in the community before or at least had never conducted
field research in these local settings. That is not true. I have been pursuing
this approach for eight years, and the results of my investigations have
consistently appeared in print, conforming to the conservative standards
of traditional scholarly article, text, and trade book writing. This time
there is a difference. Previously I had not ventured out with my mind
set to turning directly into that cognitive intersection where two problems
of postmodern organizational study meet.

Casing a Promised Land is about that intersection, the place in our
minds where the convergence of two problems central to the interpretive
mission of organizational study may be located. The first problem is all

about angles of approach to that intersection, specifically the angles created and constituted in language.

Kenneth Burke once told me that "we should not be as concerned about what we do with symbols, but with what symbols have done to us." The problem of scholarly languages, languages diverse and dichotomous, is one that lies at the heart of any interpretive study because our angle of observation—as well as what we end up observing—depends on them. It is because of this puzzle that these adventures with symbols were turned into narrative accounts.

I try to show how the problem of language enters into the interpretive experience of organizations, or more precisely, how the effects of experiencing organizations—what working in them as well as trying to observe and account for motives and behavior in them—are the central concern for studies of rhetorical communication. For me this puzzle led to the decision to create narrative accounts that reveal what symbols did to me rather than attempt to explain why they were created.

The second problem grew out of the decision to use storytelling forms and is, perhaps, more crucial to the actual accomplishment of my scholarly mission. Ever since I can remember I have wanted to be a writer, a person capable of expressing fully whatever it was that needed to be expressed, a student of the power of language and of narrative forms. This desire to become a writer alternatively led and haunted me through undergraduate and graduate schools, took me into classes on fiction and nonfiction writing, kept me up nights, and more often than not made me into a sort of mildly neurotic, verbally passionate alien, one part of my mind dangerously uncomfortable with traditional scholarly writing that I desperately needed to learn how to do, and another part of my mind yearning to be convinced that that form was basically all right because it had been for years. Besides, who was I to try to change a tradition?

So it was with some trepidation and a good bit of luck that I marched out of my doctoral studies having just completed a rhetorical biography for a dissertation in a year when most of my peers had crunched numbers. As a result I ended up taking a job at a small school in northern Alabama, safely away from the pressures of better-established programs, in a self-imposed exile in what turned out to be a unique, exotic symbolic environment.

Two things happened. First, I found out that I had landed in a universe of discourse quite unlike anything I had expected. In 1950, Huntsville, Alabama, was a cotton town with a population of about eighteen thousand, prior to the advent of Werner Von Braun and the one hundred German families that induced the city's transformation from an archetypal, Faulknerian vision of its Southern self into an international, futuristic space platform from which the future itself would be launched. Today Huntsville is home for about a quarter of a million people and claims one of the highest per capita ratios of Ph.D.s anywhere in the country. It is also the home of NASA's Marshall Space Flight Center, the U.S. Army's Missile Command, the Redstone Arsenal, over forty Fortune 500 companies, and about twelve hundred industrial and service-related firms and government agencies. For an organizational scholar, moving here was like moving into a secret promised land.

This city also offers unique opportunities and a rare appreciation for the role of communication in organizations. Huntsville was the site of the first International Conference on Organizational Communication in 1967, and the place young Phil Tompkins had come to practice his skills before moving on. Here clearly was a place where serious work could be done.

The second thing that happened was that over the course of my pretenure years I gradually learned that what constituted communication in organizations did not correspond very much to what I was reading in and contributing to scholarly journals. Most of what was actually important was being left out, not because of scholarly intentions to mask the realities of organizational life, but because the traditional forms of scholarly writing did not allow us to account for the content that we were experiencing.

At conventions and conferences I learned that I was not alone in this perception. Everyone except the hard-core numerologists admitted it, but no one seemed prepared to do anything about it. It was safer, I learned, to write articles advocating the telling of stories than to try to get a story published. The tradition was entrenched. Furthermore, among scholars of organizational culture there was a rapidly expanding, entropic universe of theoretical discourse without much fieldwork to support it. If anything, we were becoming precisely what we railed against in a previous generation of general systems theorists—users of an elaborate language code that didn't work at work.

At the 1986 Alta Summer Conference on Interpretive Approaches to Organizational Study I met Mike Pacanowsky and a band of interpretive rebels and learned that my interest in broadening the acceptance of literary forms of scholarship was widely shared. That was when I decided to get out of the office and seriously address the puzzle of narrative as scholarly writing.

Back in Huntsville I already had contacts in organizations and invitations to come in, be around, and look around. Fortunately, I also had extremely interesting organizations to examine, organizations that individually and collectively define a version of America upon which our common future will turn. This is a new promised land made out of a rhetoric of technology and hypercapitalism, a place where the future makes the news everyday.

And so became these studies. They are stories about the puzzles of experiencing organizational study. They are also about using literary narrative techniques that seek to evoke a richer, deeper sense of the experience of observing and interpreting organizational lives. Each one of them is, in its own way, a testimony to the central idea that to study an organization within a community means trafficking in its symbols and seeing connections among the individual and collective effects of those symbols on the lives that are led there.

"Becoming an Organizational Dectective" is a brief autobiographical sketch of how I moved from the role of cultural outsider to that of cultural insider within the texts and contexts of Huntsville. Stylistically, this chapter pays homage to detective mysteries because the metaphor of the detective bodies forth an image of the purposeful courting of intrigue under the guise of crime. I also use the metaphor because it allows me to experiment with forms of expression that reveal how the research process was carried out by telling stories that begin in mystery and end in at least a temporary resolution of it.

My choice of the cultural category of the detective and the corresponding literary genre of the detective mystery is based on one critical assumption and a sort of general bad feeling. First, organizational culture scholarship has taken as its task the detection of gaps in our understanding (mysteries), and our writing about organizational cultures seeks to systematically solve them (to close the case, at least temporarily). It should be pointed out here that this strategy is one of the accepted conventions of scholarly writing, conventions that reveal us as valuing our collective, formal "telling about" a culture over "showing" our readers how we have managed to immerse ourselves within them.

Hence the general bad feeling. What started out as a challenge to existing scholarship about organizations and communities increasingly looks more like it. Put simply, the forms of storytelling that began as opposition and resistance to the prevailing culture of academic writing have become absorbed, perhaps even co-opted by it. Our "literature" has been mainstreamed, rendered, well, *conventional* by the traditional forms of scholarly writing.

The detective is a person who chooses not to live a conventional life. He or she makes a living by solving other people's problems. Whether or not the problem gets solved depends on qualities of observation and interaction that lend themselves to a particular "reading" of motives, desires, relationships, processes, and people. Clues are often found, and often by accident, in unlikely places—loose threads on a carpet seen while talking to someone else about somebody else, the glint of sunlight off a golden tiepin that connects its wearer with a possible motive—and some of the most reliable information is gained by going undercover, wearing a disguise, renting an unmarked Ford. The role of the detective is that of a professional snoop, a social philosopher, and a comic actor, a person who is street-wise and willing to do what needs to be done. In choosing the prose style of a mystery writer—in my case the persona of an independent private investigator rather than the bureaucratic police lieutenant—a scholar enters into the culture of organizations armed with a sense of mystery, an attitude of healthy skepticism toward what is offered or encountered, a respect for the dignity of ordinary people, and a duty to report as fully and as completely as possible the details of the case.

This metaphor of the detective has several strategic and tactical advantages. First, it connects the life of the researcher with the subject of the study, thus allowing her or him to deal honestly with the question of interests, attitudes, and motives that surround any scholarly romance. Second, it encourages displays of intrigue and sources of mystery that are natural to any scholar's mission and permits sudden twists in the story as it is told that correspond to twists in the story as it was experienced. Third, it induces the researcher/writer to show, not tell about, that which she or he must then analyze. This tactic grounds theory in the actual, makes it tentative because it is perceptual, and favors the actors and acts, the antecedent and consequent conditions of the scene, and the various and changing ways in which symbols traffic in organizational environments over the mere theorizing about them.

In what I consider to be the best eclectic critical stance, the detective is free to use whatever tools are available to make sense of whatever is found. And what is found, at least in my experience, is a product of the detective's own responses to that culture, responses that seek to get as close as possible to actual cultural experience. It takes time, and it never quite works out the way you planned.

That said, there seems to me to be two ways in which doing organizational research from a culture perspective must account for itself to achieve some sense of authenticity. First, the detective must present the contexts of his or her prose as extensions of self and identity, the products not of neutral methods but of a lifetime of lessons, insights, judgments. Second, this telling about oneself must be done in narrative form within the context of the observations presented, a blending of self and scene into a rendering that takes into account not only what is being seen and experienced but also why this detective was induced to recognize and respond to these symbols.

These are the conceptual bases for my use of the detective metaphor. They provide a rationale for a person, acting out the investigative role of a scholar, to read the clues provided by a culture. However, such a person should also be aware that "culture" is itself a loaded term. In one sense it is a term used by bigots to make distinctions among members of a class for the purpose of highlighting their "inadequacies," a cover, really, for a desire to exclude those who don't fit in. In another sense it is a symbol used to condense the whole of lived experience as such experiences are defined and shaped by commonly held values, routines, and meanings. In this sense it is a conceptual framework, a context for a critical reading, a symbolic inducement that invites certain critical activities while ignoring (or at least repressing) others. While "culture" is but a symbol, and a symbol is a bit of magic that makes meanings the object of its enchantments, it is one that allows maximum flexibility in tracking down all that is experienced and represented within an organization or community. Culture, as symbol, encourages us to direct our critical attention—as well as to find enchantment—in what Marshall Sahlins refers to as "the meaningful orders of persons and things."

The detective, then, searches for those meaningful orders. But it is the detective writer who must represent them, locate their meanings in symbols that suggest meanings can be located in them. It is the detective writer who tells the whole story, shapes it according to some truth that came out of the experience of solving a mystery in which symbols sometimes play tricks, and sometimes don't.

When I presented this essay at the 1987 Alta Conference, Mike Pacanowsky suggested that it was a "portrait of the scholar as a young dog," which was, I suppose, his way of providing a moral for my immoral willingness to be seduced into servicing the needs of the military/industrial/high technology complex. Sometimes the detective, caught up in the pursuit of mystery, finds that he has acted very much like a partner in the crime.

The second essay focuses on culture and culture building as an exercise in the storyteller's art. "Notes on a Cultural Evolution: The Remaking of a Computer Software Company" tries to get at the ways in which everyday sensory experiences of an organization—such as the color and placement of cars in a corporate parking lot, the signs and memorabilia in offices, and the uses of inspirational speeches and informal conversations—conspire to make a culture out of shared symbols.

My friend and colleague Chris Waagen was reared on general systems theories and has what appears to be an uncanny intuition and almost mystical talent for dealing with complexity. His favorite saying is "Everything counts," which neatly sums up the multiplicity of interwoven processes and relationships that we encounter in the real world. This saying is the most important lesson a student of organizational culture can learn from a general systems orientation.

Locating meaning in an organization's culture requires paying attention to parts of the story that, while seemingly unrelated, are in fact very much part of the plot. Consider, for example, the symbolic importance of automobiles in contemporary American culture. We know, even though we don't like to admit it, that the car we drive is an emblem of our values, perhaps even of our ambitions. Why then, as students of an organization's culture particularly licensed to seek meaning in symbolic displays within that culture, don't we spend more time in parking lots? What are the possible correlations, the symbolic linkages, between the cars we drive to work and the way we think about our work when we are there? What is the relationship between the culture and its artifacts?

Similarly, we know that individuals like to define their spaces, and in organizations they tend to apply this reasoning to their workspaces, their offices. Like wolves in the wild, we mark our territories; fortunately, we use symbols instead of scents, although the jury on the effects of pheromones on human communication is still out, and manufacturers of perfumes, colognes, deodorants, and so forth do make a lot of money suggesting possibilities that may in fact figure into the true stories, particularly the romances, in organizational plots.

Here again the Rule of Waagen makes perfectly good detective sense: everything counts. In the chapter on the cultural evolution of this Boston-based computer software company, you will find that I followed this advice. My story concerns a culture that, during a particular phase of its evolution, paid very close attention to its symbolic, mostly nonverbal, displays. The structure of the story I tell is based on the formalities of a company tour, one that pauses in the parking lot before taking you into the front door, one that takes account of office symbols in the context of office politics, and one that reveals a close relationship between play and work in the building of a culture.

Read a different (and equally important) way, it is also an account of the play and work of writing about a culture. That is, finally, the partner in the lesson. The articulation of a culture is a narrative enterprise in which the symbols convey—not just to the reader but also to their author—what should happen next, what the ending should be, and what it all means. It is through the act of writing that the story becomes told; it is also through the act of creating symbols to represent a reality that a researcher learns just how much effect symbols have on our interpretations of the ultimate meaning of that reality. And that is a subject that should concern us. It may be that all scholars write fictions; we just operate out of different metaphors.

The third essay is about how the detective moves from the role of a passive insider who profits from the maintenance of a consensus reality to that of a concerned citizen who manages to penetrate an unknown, innermost dimension of that consensus reality. But of course it did not start out that way.

Huntsville is home to the U.S. Army's Star Wars Command, the place where computer simulations of the end of the world and how to prevent it are the work of its employees every day. This is one of the main reasons why Huntsville is loaded with rumors of KGB agents, rumors that are both real and imagined. So here is an organization that has as its task saving or extinguishing the human race; put delicately, how do symbols function in this environment? How is it that the ordinary individuals who work there make sense of themselves in an organizational culture whose product most of the workers believe won't work and all of them hope is never used?

This story is also an experiment in cultural representation. We have learned to say—and to accept—that stories create and reveal cultures.

This statement implies both a sort of assumed vague neutrality in the voice of the story's narrator and an absence of consideration for the attitude of the narrator toward that which is represented in the symbols of the story. However "appropriate" this neutrality and absence may be for conventional scholarly work, it has no place in interpretive studies. Interpretations are inherently tied to the "dance" of the narrator's attitude. Even more significantly, voice and attitude are ingredients in the story, responses the narrator makes to what has been seen, observed, listened to and for.

To understand the cultural life of an organization or a community— as far as true understanding can be achieved—a scholar must listen and to watch: specifically, listen to stories and watch what happens when they are told. However, you need to learn how to listen to a story and how to watch what happens when the story unfolds.

Learning to read a story is always a question of "how."

I have found that answering this question is easier said than done, given the narrow limits to what we all too commonly assume constitutes a story. For example, I used to ask students learning fieldwork methods to collect organizational stories, only to confront the inevitable disappointment summed up by the statement "I didn't hear any." The fault, of course, was more in my failure to give adequate instructions than in the students' lack of ingenuity or effort.

I have learned instead to say: "Just as every line is important to the plot of a good novel, every episode of talk is important to the overall story of an organization. Don't try to collect stories; try instead to write down complete accounts of episodes of talk that you hear—dialogue, facial expressions, body movement, silences, and so forth, as well as a description of the office space, what is on or underneath the desktops, what is hanging on the walls, where the chairs are placed, and so forth. Look for the action in the scene, but don't leave out any details because, like any good mystery, details will later become more important than they at first seem."

Mystery, although only one genre of a storyteller's art, is a good place to begin field research. A researcher just beginning to discover the semiotic and dramatic elements of a culture is analogous to a reader of a mystery: although the natural inclination is to focus on the action, there is also much to be learned from the scenes in which the action occurs. There also may be good reasons to use techniques borrowed from writers of romances, magical realism, or theaters of the absurd, but the natural beginning position of the seer in relation to the seen, the hearer in relation to what is heard, is mystery.

The second step is a bit more abstract. Fortunately, I was able to study comparative literature at the University of North Carolina under Eugene Falk, a master teacher who taught me two approaches to reading a story I have never forgotten. The first uses the natural analogy of good literature to good music, a source of comparative, narrative logic that helps a reader (or listener) learn to find meaning in rhythms, cadences, the essential "facts" of harmony and disharmony found in plot and characterization. In my memory, he did it this way:

> One day you come into a room. Let's say the room is white, although the color of the room suggests an absence of color to you. A man appears through a door and stands before you. He asks, "What does this mean?" and proceeds to voice the following four musical notes: da, da, da [pause] dum—the last note spoken lower than the rest.
> "Come on," he urges, "what does it mean?"
> You shrug. You say: "It means nothing."
> He laughs. "Nothing? Then you have no ear for music."
> You try to defend yourself: "You gave only four notes—da, da, da [pause], dum—the fourth note lower than the rest. How can that mean anything?"
> The man smiles. "You need imagination to hear music." He then clears his throat and runs the same four notes by you, only this time the first three come all at once and the fourth, lower than the rest, benefits from no pause: "Da-da-da-DUM." Instantly you recognize it as the beginning of Beethoven's Fifth Symphony.
> The room, suddenly, is full of color and meaning.

The second reading technique builds upon the logic of the first. Each note in a musical score conveys a message, a fact of itself, but it becomes part of something larger in the broader context of all of the other notes. In other words, each note suggests (to your imagination) possibilities beyond itself. In musical terms, this relationship is one of *motif* to *theme,* and the same is true of good literature. In any reasonably well-told novel, each chapter, and each line in each chapter, suggests possibilities (motifs) that contribute to the overall development of a theme.

Taken together, these two reading lessons explain the "how" of reading a story. They also help explain how to look at what constitutes the story of an organization's culture. This is because the story of an organization's culture must be articulated in a form that is part nonfiction novel (because its scenes and characters must add up to some general theme) and part music (because themes are built out of motifs, which are themselves dependent upon rhythm and voice for meaning).

The major problem for a student of organizational culture is not simply how to do research (despite our preference for courses in "research methods"), but how to write about the research. For it is in the act of writing that the theme(s) of the culture is revealed, shown rather than told, and the writing should therefore be as carefully plotted as any good novel.

Why does this problem exist?

Part of the answer is in our separation of "research methods" from "writing methods" in the way we indoctrinate initiates into the profession. Our emphasis is on research, as if it can be magically translated into prose unmediated by the experience of being human. We explain research methods in painstaking precision, direct a research project that requires hours, days, weeks of observation, and then at some point say, "Go write it up," as if the writing process has nothing to do with how the research process occurred or gets reported. We end up not telling it like it was, but like it must be if it is to reach print. The rules we have created legitimize particular ways of knowing (and writing) at the expense of others. What "counts" as knowledge of the field is relegated to sentences that have very little to do with organizations or the communication in them, but everything to do with what must be written to reach print.

Thus endeth, at least temporarily, the sermon on the nature of our professional sins.

Space is a both a controversial and contested arena in which the superpowers play. To play requires money, which in turn requires the support of taxpayers. When our local space and rocket museum (which is also "The Earth's Largest") opened its "Space Camp," it occurred to me that there may be a connection. Through a bit of luck I received an invitation to experience it, and the fourth essay here, "Lost in Space," is an account of what it is like to go through the United States Space Academy's Space Camp.

In it I try to show—through the lectures and experiences currently available to adults and children on a year-round basis—how NASA has changed from a heroic research and development organization into a government agency principally concerned with preserving its own future. My experience as a textual detective of the Space Camp message reveals a coordinated public relations activity that is—well, you'll see.

When you are reading this essay, I think it is important for you to know that I was trained in rhetorical theory and criticism. For me, rhetoric has investigative and adaptive functions. I am here referring to the Ciceronian bifurcation of the arts of invention into the discovery of the possible and the choice of the actual, as well as to his discussions of the effects of style on the audience's reception of the message. I am also referring to the work of Raymond Chandler, a writer who taught me how to appreciate the interdependence of the investigative and adaptive functions of rhetoric and who showed me that "the realistic creed which dominates our literature is not due so much to bad theories as to bad art"—a statement as true today as it was when he made it in 1912.

I point out these sources of influence here because they live in my experience of Space Camp. Being there I found myself thinking more and more like a rhetorical critic and less like an invited guest. I kept seeing the experience as a program of indoctrination and mass propaganda designed to appeal to a generation reared on slick video values that encourage us to believe that we are participating in an illusion when that illusion flashes on our screen. Sure, it's fun, but what else is it?

This story is in many ways far more straightforward than are any of the others in this collection. I tell it like it was, for me, by taking the reader step by step through the experience. However, the rhetorical critic is everywhere apparent in the way I respond to the experience, a cultural detective reading the clues according to an older script in which some of today's players also participated.

The next story builds on the insights of its predecessors, moving deeper into issues concerning what symbols do to us and for us by examining what I call the "Articles of Faith." To accomplish this essay caused the detective in me to spend many hours undercover in such places as a discount record and video store and a super mall, places that, as we shall see, seldom suffer academics gladly.

One of the writers from whom students of communication can learn a great deal is Walker Percy. A Southerner trained as a physician, he chose instead of the practice of medicine the enterprise of philosophy and contributed several essays to the learned literature before turning to novels as the fullest expression of his science and his art.

One of Dr. Percy's recurrent themes is communication between people, a theme that he uses not as a subject but as the method of his writing. In such texts as *The Moviegoer, The Last Gentleman, Love in the Ruins, Lancelot, The Second Coming,* and *The Thanatos Syndrome* he shows (rather than tells) how to read symbols, developing the reader's insight and desires to move beyond the fictional texts he has created to the broader dramatic texts of life. Reading Walker Percy is a lesson in communication, a lesson that is as well informed and studied as any first-rate scholar's, only richer through his keen ability to make a story out of it.

I was reading *The Thanatos Syndrome* and teaching textual methods of criticism (with emphasis on the writing of Stanley Fish) when I was doing the walking-around research that led to "Articles of Faith." The novel deals with a plot to deaden the self by chemical inducements to the posterior region of the cortex, to Wernicke's area, Brodmann 39 and 40, in the left brain of right-handed people, where neurologists locate the center of self-consciousness (the "I" of an utterance, and the "why" of life). I won't spoil the read for you by explaining how it turns out, but I will admit that Dr. Percy's concern for how people look when they speak and act haunted my own research and writing efforts.

What I kept coming to was an inverse Percy. In Discount Records, and in the Madison Square Mall, I saw an environment that induced not a loss of self-consciousness, but a heightened awareness of it, places where appearances and images dominated, induced not by chemical combinations but by symbolic ones. At the same time I saw presentations of self—and presentations of different social classes' responses to self as well as to this environment—as indicative of a broader historical text which mirrors in its complexity some of the concerns expressed by David Riesman in *The Lonely Crowd,* Richard Sennett in *The Fall Of Public Man,* and Christopher Lasch in *The Culture Of Narcissism.*

With these symbolic entrancements shaping my experience as an observer, participant, and critic, I approached the puzzle of writing about the self as a major player in organizational dramas in which the subject is identity.

"How I Spent My Summer Vacation" is the final story in this collection.

Scholars who spend their lives studying the cultures of organizations also exist in and contribute to the culture of their own professional organizations. This piece is about my own initial participation in one of our professional organizations, and it deals with two problems of interpretation.

First, how can a scholar who has spent a considerable amount of time studying an organization's culture in a place like Huntsville, Alabama, find the words to express that culture in the framework of a professional meeting to an audience who has not experienced the same milieu? Second, how does the culture one is addressing as a participant influence the portrayal of a culture one experienced as an observer? As you will see, these two problems intersect, and the intersection thus created becomes its own interpretive opportunity.

The writing experiment suggested by this opportunity parallels the expanding literature on "surprise and sense-making" in organizations. What can an interpretive ethnography contribute to that literature? How does the experience of a professional organization suggest meanings to newcomers? How are the bridges between the participant's past and present private and public lives constructed? How do we respond to our public identities, particularly when those public identities are formed by our contributions to the literature? How does our literature create us?

Following these essays I have included a brief account of how interpretive ethnography can be useful to organizational scholars. In it I also point out some of its pitfalls. I use this opportunity to show how the organizations I studied have changed since I studied them and to discuss how those changes would have—or should have—influenced my writing.

The issues throughout are subtle, vital ones. What do we know and how do we know it in the kingdom of organizational studies? I use the term "kingdom" purposefully to conjure up the image of a mythic environment that exists only on the printed page of what we dreamily refer to as "the literature."

For me the literature is a cultural artifact—our profession's primary one. It reveals our myths, our beliefs, our values. It also provides testimony to how we have divided our kingdom into various, often competing fiefdoms (all ruled by legends that sometimes pass for persons and persons that sometimes pass for legends), and to how courtiers (graduate students and junior faculty members) must behave themselves if they are to win tenure at court.

Ours is a sovereignty that exists only in sentences. I know this sounds like I am making a distinction between our kingdom and the world, and to tell the truth I mean to. In the world there is mystery and drama, ambiguity and action, fantasy that is insightful and reality that is mundane. People have faces, facial expressions, tics. They have bodies. They work in offices that have goofy artifacts they take seriously and serious objects they think are goofy. They wear clothing and strut their colognes, adopt poses. Sometimes they wish they were doing something else, which, when they think about it, they are. They drive cars and trucks whose colors are important to them, whose stereos play music that evokes in them the need to sing. Out loud. Off key. Or, sometimes, perfectly.

They also come equipped with motives and desires. If you spend enough time with them—the amount being entirely dependent on your relationship—they may tell you about them. When they do, they speak in voices that are never neutral, voices that suggest more, or less, than they are saying. Oddly enough, communication researchers have known all of this for years. The research has been done, arguments made. What is left is the translation of those understandings into the practical language of the everyday.

This is where good interpretive ethnography enters the scene. Unfortunately, it also tends to make the ethnographer look like an anarchist in the kingdom.

What is good interpretive ethnography?

To answer this question we must step outside the fiefdom of organizational communication and move into the territories claimed by some noted authorities in the fields of anthropology, folklore, and sociology. In doing so we also gain a perspective on the origins of fieldwork and the ways in which individual personalities and writing styles influence our reading of a culture and its symbols.

The practice of ethnography—which means, basically, representing in words what you have lived through as a person when your stated purpose was to study a culture—has a variety of beginnings, depending on whose history you read and what intellectual baggage you carry into that reading. If you pledge allegiance to the discipline of anthropology you trace your roots back to Darwin-like early and mid-nineteenth century accounts of the savages from the perspective of the civilized, and pay homage to Joseph-Marie Dégerardo (1800). Historians may take issue with this, however, and explain to you that Herodotus was the first ethnographer. European anthropologists favor Bronislaw Malinowski, who, you will remember, was under house arrest by the British during World War I and found himself tenting on a South Pacific island with the Trobriand natives he later wrote about. Americans favor Franz "Papa" Boas, who is often credited with encouraging scholars to get out of their lecture halls more often.

I also acknowledge a debt to F. Scott Fitzgerald and Franz Kafka. Fitzgerald, principally through his famous naive narrator, Nick Carraway, does essentially the same thing, albeit with a good bit more literary style, in his uncovering of the layers of deception among the rich, in the unpacking of symbols extent in his end of the twentieth century, and in his learning about Jay Gatsby and what he represents. The result is a novel treatment of an intersection of a particular culture that reveals how symbols function to create and sustain social order, unite and divide individuals, and stand as emblems to the everyday penetrations that the public sphere makes on the private life. It is a literary masterpiece, but it also makes excellent interpretive ethnography.

Franz Kafka's *The Castle* or *The Trial* should similarly be required reading for organizational scholars intrigued by the potential of ethnography. In both novels we are presented with an ordinary soul confronted with extraordinary circumstances—and these extraordinary circumstances are nothing less than bureaucracy. I do not know of any other work that so completely depicts the helplessness or dependence fostered by this style of organizational knowing, nor do I know of one that serves as so brilliant a critique of it.

Our task as scholars in general and ethnographers in particular is to write sentences that fairly represent the realities we have experienced. It is also to make the reading of that reality accessible to others who have not seen it and who must rely on our guidance to share in it. Our task, then, is to communicate.

The problem is not that we are blind. We are encouraged to go out in the organizations of America and *observe,* but what are we encouraged to *see?* It seems to me that we are bound by the limited rationality of ritualized observation, constrained by traditions of learning about the research process that call into serious question our desire to advance knowledge. If what we know is found in the sentences that form our collective literatures, and our literatures are constrained by a preference for conventional discussions of research methods over experimentation with writing methods, then how can new knowledge be generated? How can challenges to the way we know be accommodated by conventional forms of expression?

Let me borrow an analogy here first articulated by Martá Calas and Linda Smircich. Our research tradition is one of a decidedly modernist historical and epistemological framing. It is akin to the realistic tradition that dominated the fields of art and architecture at the turn of the century. Modernism and realism are related because as forms of expression they focus on function, the overt, and the obvious. In art and architecture they were resisted and then opposed outright by surrealism, a form of expression that valued the interpretive over the real, the nuanced and subtle over the traditions that held no language or format for these changes.

Interpretive ethnography, as a form of expression, as a way of knowing, and as a challenge to the existing wisdom of scholarship, is much like surrealism. What we have here is a source of resistance and opposition to a tradition that will not, cannot, be easily accommodated. It does not depict the same world because it does not see the same world.

The central issue here is not one of simply challenging the status quo. After all, scholars—like other artists—rarely change their minds. They do not practice their prose in a particular way simply because it is "the way things are done." They *believe* in it; they are convinced their performances of scholarship are correct. What they write, and the way they write, does fit the world they live in.

For interpretive ethnographers, however, there is increasingly an "otherworld" that can neither be captured nor fairly represented in traditional scholarly forms. Perhaps, as Stephen Tyler asserts, this is because we see a postmodern world that seriously calls into question the epistemological premises that guide Western traditions of thought. Perhaps it is because our experience of meanings in organizations and communities comes to us only in the stories we tell about them, and so the ways we read ourselves into those stories become the investigative means we need to articulate if our aim is to tell the truth. Or perhaps it is something else, an ineffable enchantment with the magic of words, the knowing that comes only from the doing when the doing is writing and the knowing is finally expressed.

Whatever it is, and for whatever reason these conditions of discourse exist as an issue in diverse intellectual communities at this particular historical moment, what is happening to the writing of scholarship is worthy of our serious attention. Interpretive ethnography is ultimately not the message, merely the messenger.

Casing a Promised Land

1

Becoming an Organizational Detective

It was a matter of chance that I should have rented a house in one of
the strangest communities in North America.
—F. Scott Fitzgerald, *The Great Gatsby*

What you've got here, really, are *two* realities, one of immediate
artistic appearance and one of underlying scientific explanation, and
they don't match and they don't fit and they don't really have much
of anything to do with one another. That's quite a situation. You
might say there's a little problem here.
—Robert Persig, *Zen and the Art Of Motorcycle Maintenance*

You get out of the old school and move into the New South. You
drive the U-Haul, wife and cat follow in the Renault. You turn off the
interstate in lower Tennessee onto a two-lane blacktop that without
mercy drops you into northern Alabama's cankerous lip. For the next
thirty miles you glance eagerly into rearview mirrors and see your wife's
expression turn from hopeful optimism into a struggle for control over
a basic instinct to flee. This is not the land you promised her; this is not
even a land you believed still existed. This is poor: narrow, shoulderless,
potholed roads lined with rotting wooden two-room rusty tin-roofed
shacks peopled by thin or fat ambivalent blacks, front porches crumbling
down under the weight of ancient washing machines, broken sofas, and
swarms of children.

A sign welcomes you to Hollywood. Another proclaims that this is
Alabama the Beautiful. The narrow road widens into a broad, modern,
divided four-lane; to the left rise the two tall towers of a nuclear power
plant. There are no more shacks, no more blacks, no more children. You
glance again into the rearview mirror and see a signature of disappointment, mostly around her eyes.

It is night as you drive over the last hill into Huntsville. An army of
lights from the valley sparkle up at you through a steamy haze, your
radio tells you it is 8:45 P.M. and the temperature is still ninety-three
degrees. This is the Rocket City, the town Von Braun built, your new

home. You pass miles of common fast-food restaurants and glitzy car dealerships engulfed in fast, maddening traffic. You get lost and have to ask for directions from a man who speaks a language with only occasional use of vowels. The first words your wife speaks are: "My God, this looks like the worst parts of northern New Jersey!"

Where are you?

You move in, unpack, go out, unpack again. This seems to go on for days.

On a Saturday at the end of your first week a drunk pounds on your door at 2 A.M. and demands Sheila. You grab an umbrella and shout back at him from the other side of the front door. "There is no Sheila here!"

"Bullshit!" He pounds on the door again. "Sheila tol' me ta come, gave me this 'dress." He staggers backward. "Said I could have a *real* good time."

"Sheila lied. Nobody's having a good time here."

This seems to satisfy him. He falls down the steps, gets up, and disappears into the darkness caused by the absence of a streetlight.

The next morning you discover your car stereo has been stolen. You take comfort only when you see your neighbor's tires have been slashed. The police tell you there is nothing you can do. They say they hope you have insurance.

There is a party for new faculty at Echols Hill, the president's estate in the heart of the antebellum district downtown.

You remember thinking last spring, when they flew you in for an interview, that everyone lived like that. This was before you fully understood the difference between night and day, as in the salary differences between you and the engineers.

You and your wife dress up and go.

There are more parties. You go together, feeling like detectives caught up in some undefinable case in which the central mystery is you.

You begin looking for clues:

1. A softer, subtler idiom is passed among women in white cottons and linens who are uniformly beautiful and bright and distanced from lesser polyester richer men who cling together uncomfortably, smoking

nodding joking, away from practiced party manners and classical muzak. At parties the men work on each other, the women wait upon the men.

2. This is the valley of secrets, and promises, and money. The secrets lead to promises, and the promises supposedly lead to money.

3. The talk of men has no past. Every word is a gamble, every story is a hedge against an uncertain future too green too simple and undoubtedly true. No one believes a word of it, of course. For this is not a language of belief, not a conversation woven out of fine words where every pleat and cut of the vocabulary is designed for a neat tailored fit, but a functional language where it is okay to sew expletives into the fabric of old clichés. The expletives are numbers with dollar signs, and there is no melody, no rhythm, no rhyme, and nothing to remember, just big, dumb numbers standing out in plain sentences. These are the terms of future agreements, hard contract talk, ways to romance grants out of innocent agencies, the first names of people to talk to, and hints of impending fortunes.

You think: This is the pitched language of high-pressure salesmen who call what they do the "new entrepreneurial spirit." I sense in that high-sounding phrase just a new breed of pirates, con artists, tycoons, and thieves for whom money is the common object of desire, the comaker (along with luck) of an unutterable dream called happiness.

4. They never talk about what they do when they talk about making money. They just make money.

5. Everybody looks like they are enjoying this; underneath probably nobody is.

6. Talk that matters: Money, looks, politics, sports, the ability to say one thing and mean another.

7. Talk that doesn't matter: Education, books, art (except as a possession), music, automobiles (except as signs of wealth or prestige), intelligent conversation, religion, ethnic background, liberal causes.

You are at another party looking for clues. Your wife whispers that this grand antebellum mansion is owned by young newlyweds.

You are young, newlyweds. You live in a small apartment with pine board bookshelves and a mattress on the floor. Your neighbors include a folksinger cynic who lacks everything except a profound talent for the same three chords and a night-screaming nymph with a boyfriend named CHARLIEEEEEEEEEEEOHHHHHGODDDDD!!!

You own a shiny new Ph.D. In this community that owns more of them per capita than anywhere outside of Cambridge, it is pronounced "phud." Rhymes uncannily with dud, mud. Ahh, but if those years of romantic educational self-indulgence have taught you anything, they have taught you that the future of America belongs to the well educated. First, however, you must learn how to use it.

You teach three sections of public speaking to people who would rather not and one section of interviewing to people who do it for a living for companies that have already sent them through the fancy training seminars on the subject you've only read about.

In your office, which until yesterday consisted of a hospital bed and a telephone because it was the first aid station, you explain to the bleeding, lost, and feverish your desire to write a good book. Coming in search of bandages, direction, and aspirin, they are inevitably disappointed.

You live, of course, to research and write, which you pursue despite the fact that most of the already meager resources of the library are on reserve for senior members of the business faculty and the journals you've been brought up adoring are, as the librarian tells you, "absent and without hope of acquisition."

He sighs.

You sigh.

You join the local literary association and gain access again to the splendid homes of Huntsville. For entire afternoons you and your wife are happy. This is, of course, because you are pretending to be rich and famous and because with increasing frequency you drink a little too much.

It dawns on you, like an angry hangover, that none of these people are academically talented although almost all of them have degrees. When you are asked, finally, by one of them to conduct a workshop on "effective communications" (*sic*) you leap at the chance to make a little extra money. You figure that what you have to say is worth about fifty dollars and spend it mentally on a really good meal for you and your wife.

They offer $3000 and suggest that if it isn't enough to let them know. Something can be worked out.

You are unable to breathe. Your wife is jumping up and down clapping, happy. That night from your playful neighbor comes the inevitable night scream "CHARLIEEEEEOHGODDDDD!!!" and for the first time you both think this is very funny.

One thing leads into another. You do it for the money and the money is good, although with each course, each seminar, each retreat, it feels less so.

Some days you feel like a whore. Other days, you act like one. You remember thinking badly of all that contract talk and wonder what has happened to you. Pirates suddenly don't seem so bad. Tycoons can be a positive force in society. Con artists and thieves are the romantic subjects of popular films.

You prefer to think of yourself as a modern day sophist and tell your students that sophists, in general, got a bad rap.

In the end you squander the money.

You leave the apartment for an old house, not quite antebellum but old and full of potential. You buy a new car. Your wife goes to work at a computer firm and when you complete your income tax it occurs to you that your combined income is more than your father ever made in his life. And your father did well.

You have an old guy for a neighbor and his name is Verbal Dodge. He is retired, a real engineer, the kind of old guy who comes over and knows how to fix everything, which makes you feel like you don't know anything that matters and you're the one with the grand education.

Afternoons he takes up residence in the broad shade of his front porch and you take it as an invitation to talk with him. One day he asks you what you do when you do "organizational communication consulting" and you have an incredibly difficult time explaining it to him. You talk about metaphors of organizational design. You analyze organizational cultures. You write about Kenneth Burke's theories of symbol use and abuse in organizational settings.

"You mean to tell me that people pay money for that?" He winks at me. "Oh my."

You press on. You say you conduct workshops on managerial communication, group leadership, and presentational speaking and writing for executives.

He nods. He lights his pipe, unimpressed.

"Well," I say confronted with the truth of it from his perspective, "companies need to know that."

He thinks about this for a while. A light wind comes up and brushes against the leaves. He tells you a story: "When I was in the army during the war we ended up in Belgium. We were in the Corps of Engineers, so we had lots of heavy equipment. The order came down for us to bury it instead of shipping it back home. Some consultant said it would be cheaper. So we did it."

"You *buried* heavy equipment?"

"That's right. Millions and millions of dollars worth of it."

"That doesn't seem right."

"That's what we thought. We told our commanding officer but he didn't want to hear about it. So we went out one night and told the local farmers where it was going to be buried and promised them that we would service the equipment and line it up right so that once they dug it back up everything would work."

"That's wonderful," I say.

"It seemed like the right thing to do. I mean, they had a use for it."

"Did you tell your commanding officer about it?"

"Oh no! We couldn't have done that."

"Why not?"

"Because he wouldn't have understood. It was too practical and besides it was technically against orders."

"That's too bad," I say, thinking about the failure to communicate.

Verbal looked directly at me. "Maybe. Maybe not. Look, what you do is tell the bosses how to talk about the work, which in my experience means how not to do any of it. But who tells the people who do the work anything? Nobody. They have to figure it out for themselves, and if they tell the bosses the bosses will tell them that it's wrong.

"What you need to do is get in there with the people who do the work and find out what really goes on. Then *you* can tell the bosses. Then you'd really be doing something worthwhile."

His words were true.

You notice that you and your wife are invited to an increasing number of socially correct events.

You wonder why. You still don't make very much money, nor do you live in a fashionable part of town. When you tell people you teach "communication" at the university, they still ask why or what *that* is.

You attribute your social success to your wife, who is beautiful, smart, and kind. She also works in the computer business, which is something people seem to instantly understand despite the fact that nobody really talks about what they do there. You gain some small acceptance as her escort primarily because you have learned to say that you are a consultant who writes books (which you have), which in this community is roughly akin to being a whore with memoirs.

People always want to know how much money you make at it, whether you'll take on any new customers, how confidential the whole affair will be. You aren't easy, you tell them, but some firms do take advantage.

You avoid telling them what exactly you do, which is train people who make many times as much money as you do to speak in a clear, organized, and concise manner. Sometimes this means helping them overcome a tendency to drool, to turn around and face the audience instead of the blackboard, and to say early on in a talk that "there are three ways to examine this problem" before explaining those three ways.

But these are not words you want to say out loud in public when people ask you what you do. Instead you find yourself talking about money, giving out the first names of people to talk to, getting into the entreprencurial spirit.

Your big break comes when you are asked in a consulting job to solve an organizational communication problem. You work day and night for a month collecting data, interviewing workers, figuring and refiguring. You agonize over the findings, how you can present the managers with the results.

Some big part of this puzzle is missing.

You feel you aren't seeing the whole truth, or perhaps, nothing but it. You know organizations are made up of smaller individual truths, most of which are disconnected.

You have been finding all the clues, but now you figure out that you don't know how to read them.

You have been hitting Raymond Chandler novels pretty hard. One afternoon on a lark you dress up as a worker and drive to the plant in the old Plymouth four-door Whale and walk in, as if to apply for a job. The receptionist appraises your style of dress, avoidance of eye contact, unkempt hair, general character, and does not return your smile.

"What if a man wanted to apply for a job?" you ask, faking your intentions and an accent that sounds, when you deliver it, surprisingly authentic.

She hands you a form and tells you to sit down and fill it out, asks if you read and write and suspects out loud that you don't own a pencil.

You get as far as your name and address and phone number. The rest makes about as much sense as your last tax form. You are supposed to know, by rote, not only your entire employment history, including mailing addresses and zip codes, but also the dates, the names of your supervisors, salaries, and so on. You quietly leave the plant with the form.

Your next stop is the machine shop. This is the place where dead chickens are shot at window glass at 635 miles per hour, a procedure known in the industry as "the bird test." You are still in your work clothes but introduce yourself to the foreman as a writer interested in doing a piece on the plant. He is friendly and introduces you around.

You observe firsthand how communication occurs in this test site. Mostly there is noise, a lot of it, created by the cannons that fire the chickens at the window glass. There is also the fact that everyone wears hearing-protection devices, an OSHA requirement. Measurements are taken, forms are filled out.

You ask the foreman how he presents the results of the tests to the managers. He grins. "I just send it along to them, sometimes with a note."

"Do you talk with them about what goes on down here?"

"Naw." He looks perplexed. "A waste of time. They only want to see the numbers."

"What do you think they do with them?"

He shrugs. "Don't know."

You do this sort of thing for another week. You change clothes, drive different cars, hedge your way around the truth of the inquiries without actually ever telling a bold-faced lie.

You are learning how to read.

You write up your report.

The managers are surprised and a little uncomfortable. "How did you do this?" you are asked. "How did you find this out?"

You explain your methods with Chandlerian precision. You tell them a story with clues that seemingly don't connect, then you connect them and the rest is obvious. You tell them that you were hired to do a job, and sometimes that job requires extreme methods.

You present a plan for change that includes bringing the foreman into the management meetings and reducing the noise level in the shop. You show them a revised hiring form that reads easily and doesn't require a college education to complete. You tell them that every salesperson should be required to work through the entire production process and that supervisors and foremen should be required to attend at least one sales presentation a year to see what kinds of objections and complaints are raised and to see what can be done to overcome them.

They like these ideas very much. They ask you what they should call this innovative management style.

You smile. You tell them, "Call it 'the Good Neighbor.' " You are, of course, thinking of Verbal Dodge.

You have learned that an organization, like your own identity, is best approached as a mystery.

The answers are always in the reading.

You have learned also that mystery writers often provide sound methods for consultants.

For the next few years you apply what you have learned.

You receive a promotion at the university, then tenure. You author more books, articles.

You acquire more money. You refurnish the house, buy a new computer, a stereo system, an old MGA, an old Porsche 911, and always more books. On your birthday your wife gives you a pair of golden retriever puppies, and you decide the time might be right to move to the country.

You and your wife buy a horse, a tractor, another horse, and move out to the country.

All appears well.

Homer Bright is your new neighbor.

Past seventy and stout, he is as strong as the white oaks he helps you cut down to rebuild your barn. He helps you because he wants to, and he won't take any money for it although you do eventually convince him to take off your hands an old tractor that he has several times admired.

His job, you will learn, although you will learn it slowly and the learning at times will be painful, is to teach you how to improve your reading. He will accomplish this simply by telling you stories, letting you draw your own conclusions.

You will listen to them.

You will think about them.

You will ask questions about why they are being told, and especially why they are being told to you. You will not, however, be able to ask

Homer any of these questions. These are not questions suited to a storyteller. They are the questions a listener, an observer, a reader of texts and subtexts and contexts asks. They are questions born in mystery and compelled by a sense of scholarly romance, questions that appreciate the subtle and the nuanced over the overt and obvious, questions that value the meanings of truth over the collection of facts.

They begin, of course, with some clues.

Homer defines this space known on the map as northern Alabama as "this country," a phrase that, as he pronounces it, *is* the whole world and he lives as its spokesman. He tells you there is a lot to learn about this country.

You know you are an immigrant new to this country, a resident on a quiet lane that goes by the name of School House Road, despite the fact that, as Homer has it, there never was a schoolhouse on it. To him you are a person who must be educated about its past to gain real citizenship in it, citizenship being defined as a formal invitation to join the Thatch Volunteer Fire Department or to become a member of the Piney Woods Baptist Church.

But first there is much you must acquire.

You think: This is like grammar. Or the parts of speech. You are learning a vocabulary capable of defining centers of meaning.

You begin at the house you just bought, a house that comes equipped with a history.

This is the house that Homer built at the edge of his property for his daughter, gave it to her on her wedding day. But she married a man who gambled and drank, and he lost it in a game when his two pair did not beat another man's three of a kind.

True story.

One hundred thousand dollars bet on two pair. Imagine that.

The house, perhaps as a result, has certain characteristics. For instance, every man who has lived here has gone to seed, something you did not learn until after you'd signed all the papers.

After Homer's son-in-law there was a second owner who bought it from the gambler who won it in the card game. This man was rumored to have embezzled money from a business which caused him to lose his job, which caused him to turn up the flames on his drinking, which caused his marriage to burn. He is the man you bought the house from, a man you had to buy a six-pack for just to keep him cool through the closing. It was a sign and you should have read it as such.

But that was before Homer began teaching you how to read the signs in this country.

You are worried by this revelation. And you would be a liar if you said it didn't also worry your wife. But there is so much beauty out here, so much promise. You take it as a challenge to keep on the straight and narrow in a house where otherwise good men consistently seem not to.

For some reason you find yourself playing "Walk Like a Man" a lot. Getting regular haircuts. Avoiding bad language.

One excellent evening when you are led to believe that God has a fine eye for the details of color because of the vivid brushstrokes that are at that moment a blue and violet sky, you drive home behind the wheel of a new silver Corvette. Your wife tolerates this obvious excess of the consumer spirit, despite the fact that she dislikes, as she puts its, "what a Corvette suggests, particularly about the man who drives it." Only later does Homer explain to you that each of the other two men who lived in your house also purchased silver Corvettes. You are seized by an unnameable panic.

You don't know why.

For days you are haunted by it. Within a few weeks you begin to tell everyone that your Corvette is not silver, but *gray*. In a few months it is gone entirely, sold at a low price on account of what it stands for.

Among the men, you can blame your wife. She never liked the car. With your wife, you can only blame yourself. You were a fool. Alone, you wonder about the other men who lived in this house and who bought, and sold, silver Corvettes.

Perhaps this is a consequence of learning how to read.

You are comforted when you are told, by Homer, that this house was built to withstand any weather.

Homer is a weather reporter, a predictor of things to come, a talent he has picked up over the years in this country. It is a talent for reading subtle shifts of wind, the thicknesses of coats on certain breeds of caterpillars, the habits of squirrels. He knows that in this country the weather can come in fast and hard, ice and snow and cold followed by balmy days when the temperature in December reaches the mid-seventies. The house stands in "Tornado Alley," a wide region of northern Alabama that suffers about twenty heavy-duty sky attacks a year. So when he built this house for his daughter he made it strong, a white brick Cape Cod storm shelter with glacier insulation, two complete heating systems, and a big fireplace just in case.

Back when he was in business, he built shopping centers. So when he decided to put air conditioning in this house he ordered up a five-ton unit for a Winn-Dixie grocery store. With pride he tells you that it would be safe to "hang meat" in the kitchen if it came to that.

He leaves the "it" in that last sentence strangely undefined.

So do you.

Now to the yard and the acreage and the stories narrated by Homer Bright.

There are thirty-seven oak trees in your front yard, another thirty or so in the pasture. If the economy turns sour, Homer says, you'll always have wood for heat. Up the lane where Homer lives in a red-brick mansion is his own log pile that reaches, by early autumn, to an intimidating height, cut by his own hand from his own forest, a fact which brings you to the events that led to your first reading lesson in the class of one, taught by Mr. Bright.

> You are cutting wood together, chain saws and the occasional axe, when he pauses to tell you about the couple that lived in a small house down in the forest he now owns. You cut off your engine to listen.
> He begins: "It came a hard winter, man I mean hard. This fella hadn't cut enough wood and caught a cold, died of pneumonia before the weather broke. His wife was a frail woman, a good woman, kind. But being frail all she could do was drag him out the house and leave him on the front porch. Then she went back in the house and died too. I found them myself one morning when no smoke rose from their little chimney down there in the woods. It was a sad thing. Man, that winter was cold."

That is a Homer story about how it was. He never says exactly when it was, and you have learned not to ask. There is a clear and compelling moral to his stories, although he never articulates them.

Call it reading a subtext, if you want to.

In the above hard-winter story he tells you how important it is to be prepared for anything. *Anything*. There is something about this country that makes anything possible, even likely. You are situated in it, and as you acquire its language, constructed by it too.

Fighter jets soar overhead, and they aren't always ours.

What does this mean? Or better, what *can* this mean?

Perhaps you need another story. Perhaps you need to be reminded where you are.

And that your task is to learn how to read.

> You are lowering the roof on one side of your barn. You are lowering it because, according to Homer, the man who originally built it drank to the point that his wife left him and he no longer knew that rainwater wouldn't run uphill, and so when rain falls on the roof it has nowhere to go, nothing to do except rot the roof and run into the horse stall, which annoys the horse a good bit.
>
> So you are lowering the roof, much to horse's delight.
>
> Homer stopped his work for a moment and pointed over across the lane to a small grove of trees. He said that one of his cousins used to live over there with a man who drank. Then the man started running around with other women, women who drank [and who, by implication of a certain gaze he gives you, did other things that Christian men didn't need to mention]. The woman took it until she couldn't take it any longer. So she saved up her money, by the nickel but mostly by the penny, and did what she did.
>
> "What was that, Homer?"
>
> "Killed herself. Right over there one morning in that woods."
>
> "That's awful, Homer."
>
> "Yes, it was. The man was laid up drunk somewhere and didn't know it for two-three days."
>
> You have to ask it. "How did she do it? With a gun?"
>
> "Naw. Man, she didn't use no gun. Wouldn't have known how to use no gun."
>
> You do not think you want to pursue this, but he goes right on anyway.
>
> "She saved her money up and bought lye, drank it right over there in those woods."
>
> Some silences have a weight there are no words to describe.
>
> "She was a good woman, too. Never hurt anybody."
>
> Finally, after fighting back the ugly boiling sickness at the back of your throat, you reenter the common world of words. You say, "Her life must have been pretty bad to make her want to drink lye."
>
> "Well, she never said. Hold that post while I crank this roof down."

If you are thinking that there is a lot of death going on here, you are right. That is a fact.

But where is the truth? What are these facts spelling out, making into sentences? What are they saying that is greater than they are?

Remember, you are learning how to read. Homer is the teacher.

Two more jets soar overhead. You hear them, but do not see them, and then they are gone. An old blue truck crawls down School House Road. In it is a toothless neighbor who waves, smiles. You smile, wave.

You watch his truck round the corner. You watch him, but you are thinking about the jets. Were they ours?

Another story, same theme, different person:

You are both standing in your driveway, the one that he built between the rows of oaks for a dream of happiness he wished upon his daughter but the wish didn't come true. It is Sunday morning, and it is his ritual to come down and stand in the driveway with you and talk. Summers he brings fresh vegetables from his garden, winters he brings predictions on the weather.

You have learned to listen, in this country, for clues.

You ask him about the man who drives the old blue pickup truck at precisely five miles per hour everywhere around here. He tells you the man is a Fitt but this could be a name or an insult so you ask for clarification.

"Ol' Coy Fitt, that's who it is. He's harmless. He drinks so he drives slow, that's all. He wouldn't hurt nobody. He had a bad daddy growing up and in some ways he turned out just like him."

You think this is going to be another one of Homer's drinking stories, don't you? And you call yourself a detective. You still haven't learned a thing.

"Why, his daddy used to lay up drunk and then get mean, come down the mountain and stand all ten of his children up against a fence and swear he was going to shoot them. Almost every Friday night."

"Jesus." You are imagining this in a way that lets you know it was close to how it was, ten scared faces and a lunatic with a gun.

"But Ol' Coy got even with him. At least some say it was Coy. I don't know."

He knows. Somehow, so do you.

You have to ask it. "What happened?"

"The old man came down the mountain with the gun but passed out in his bed before he could do anything with the children. So Coy or one of them put the daddy's finger on the trigger and then made some kind of wild noise in the house so that when the old man jumped he pulled the trigger on himself. Bullet went plumb through him, through the bed, through the floor."

"Killed him? You mean they killed him?"

"Well. Depends on how you look at it. He pulled the trigger on his ownself and there wasn't nobody in this country willing to say any different."

"You mean that man that drives by my house every day killed his own father?"

"Don't be too hard on ol' Coy, now. He's a good fella. He might not live the way you and I do but he carries a lot inside of him."

You guess so. You know you will never be able to see that truck again in the same way. Jets or no jets.

You have learned that you live in a country defined by wicked men and sudden death, a beautiful, lush country that seems willing to reveal its deepest secrets. In the center is a narrator named Homer Bright, a moralist and a Christian man.

This is in Alabama, but you already know that, and it lies only a few miles as measured on any map from the high technology of another place called Huntsville. You think of this every time a jet fighter soars over your property, suggesting connections that you cannot yet name, or an old blue truck rumbles by your house, naming things you do not want to suggest, in this, in this *country*.

Maybe now you are ready to go into town and look around. Maybe you have to.

2

Notes on a Cultural Evolution: The Remaking of a Software Company

The merits of American style are less numerous than its defects and annoyances, but they are more powerful. . . . It is more alive to cliches. Its impact is emotional and sensational rather than intellectual. It expresses things experienced rather than ideas.

—Raymond Chandler's working notebook

A corporation which decides to rebuild its image has decided less on a change of heart than on a change of face.

—Daniel Boorstin, *The Image*

GOING IN

You cross a sewer drainpipe to get there.

Lately, the ditch where the sewer water runs has been the final resting place of a rusted Winn-Dixie shopping cart, an artifact no doubt stolen from the nearby Winn-Dixie Plaza, which features (in addition to the Winn-Dixie) an Emergency Clinic, a Buy Wise discount drug store, a Radio Shack, a Buy Rite discount shoe store, a European Tanning Spa, a Hills' discount department store, and one of those afternoon saloons without windows, the kind of purely functional dive that might, if you walk into it, change forever your views on the nature of things.

This plaza and all that it suggests is so far removed psychologically from the ultra-high-tech research park that squares off against it from across a four-lane highway that the visual symbol of the overturned shopping cart in the ditch by the regional office of a Boston-based computer software company (B-BCSC) is disturbing. Even more disturbing is the bright red- and-white message printed on the cart that, because of the angle of its overturn, faces everyone who drives into the parking lot: "We want to help you do things right!"

Maybe it is the presence of the ditch on the way into this company, or maybe it is the message on the shopping cart lodged in the ditch that you had to pass over to get into the parking lot, or maybe it is the contrast of the whole thing, knowing that here in America, in a

16

deeply Southern part of America that truly represents what a flood of defense contracts can do for a cotton town over the space of twenty or thirty years, a Boston-based computer software firm with great expectations can be housed in a place you can only get to by crossing over a drainage ditch, passing by a rotting abandoned thing with a message too real to be ignored, too ironic to be forgotten—maybe this is why you spend time in the parking lot to begin with, maybe to collect yourself, maybe to search for meanings in the essential patterns of everyday experience.

You can learn to ask questions about the culture of an organization by examining the contents of its parking lot.

This is particularly true if the organization in question is actively concerned with building an image or is making a serious attempt to develop a culture. We have known for some time now that nonverbal communication predates and precedes other forms, and it is reasonable to assume that in organizations where culture is the issue, this may also be true.

The cars you pass in the B-BCSC parking lot are artifacts of the interchange of traffics public and private, and they do, both singularly and collectively, suggest realities whose appearances are of primary cultural importance: Honda, Chevrolet, Buick, Toyota, another Honda, another Honda, another Buick, a Fiat, a small Ford truck. And so on. Nothing is very much older than a forty-eight month note could purchase, and there are no motorcycles, bicycles, or multicolored Volkswagen micro-buses.

These are the cars and light trucks of aspiring, mostly boom-generation professionals who derive a way of knowing and being from the office that often follows them home. In an older generation this might have been called an identity, separated into its corporate and individual components, analyzed for its dependence on the status of the work or the prestige of the firm. But for this generation *identity* is too large and too stable a term to describe the movement of roles we enact and functions we carry out, the intricate interplays of working and living, the changes in attitude or values that circumstances adapt us to. Ways of knowing, ways of being, ways of doing, ways of seeing contribute to purposes more fluid than identities can catch.

Perhaps this is why a parking lot with only three red vehicles in it, and nothing vaguely exotic, not even a four-wheel drive, attracts attention, appeals to the sense of mystery that any cultural investigation begins with. There is much strategic ambiguity passing for beige and light blue and off-white on cars that are uniformly protected by optional side moldings. They rest just on either side of the B-BCSC building, straight rows of muted colors suggesting some sort of pattern.

Culture is a term we apply first to patterns of traffic, then to patterns of symbols that move the traffic into meaningful experiences. In the traffic patterns created by the experience of organization, some symbols stand out and are easily read. What stands out is the exception more often than the rule. For instance, in America, Corvettes receive far fewer speeding tickets than Porsches despite the obvious fact that there are many more of them, and the people that buy them drive them just as fast. But troopers are typically patriotic, and the Corvette is America's true sports car. To ticket a Corvette is to turn against apple pie; to ticket a Porsche is to eat it and order up a second slice. The fact that the Porsche is foreign is not the whole point of the story. Dodges receive tickets, so do other Chevrolets, so do Fords.

What stands out is the meaning of the symbol, its natural appeal, with which we either identify or do not. Looking at the cars in the B-BCSC parking lot I am reminded of an archaelogical truth: the more ordinary the object, the less likely it will be preserved, and yet, in terms of the culture producing it, the more meaningful it will be. The meaning of a cultural symbol, an ordinary artifact, poses an essential question: Is this the exception or is it the rule?

Max Weber pointed out that the concept of culture includes both "consciousness of kind" and "consciousness of difference," an insight that attains special importance when we consider that "culture" is a term we generally reserve for others, who, for whatever reason, are discovered to be "different" from ourselves. To understand a culture requires an appreciation of both integration and differentiation of symbols, how the traffic patterns created by them move and how its movement is understood by those caught in it.

For these reasons, my investigation of B-BCSC's culture began in a parking lot, a place where symbols generally regarded to be significant in America are parked, a place on Sparkman Drive that reveals only three red cars out of a possible ninety, a subtlety perhaps that brought me into this investigation.

Two of the three red cars are driven by women, both of whom are supervisors, both of whom are attractive, both of whom are married, and both of whom are thirty-three.

One of the red cars is a Renault Alliance purchased at a Hertz sale for a price well below book value. The woman who owns it calls it "her little red car" in a voice that most of us reserve for children under the age of three. For her, the car is an inferior thing, just a practical machine, something cheap with a fair stereo and the necessary air conditioning. She is an artist from a working-class background, a woman with a doctorate in education who found that a job in corporate training not only offered more money, but also allowed her the time to pursue her "other" career as a weaver.

These values are, for her, core values, easily accessed by asking questions about her decision to purchase a car, a red car called an Alliance. They are values that apply equally well to her attitude toward work ("I work because I want to be paid well for what I do, and my weaving, which is my real work, doesn't pay well at all"), her management style ("People should be honest and direct; the most important thing is to get the job done"), and, to some extent, the degree to which she is willing to share in the culture of the company ("I do what I have to do, but this is not my whole life.") She drives a practical car.

By contrast, the other woman who drives a red car wishes it was blue. She wishes she still had the blue Quantum her husband foolishly traded in last September for this red Jetta GLI, the car she simply refers to as "the Volkswagen." To her, this car is a temporary means of transportation, not a vehicle to get close to, because soon she will trade it in on either a Porsche, a Volvo, or a small Mercedes. She drives another vehicle to work more often these days—a red Toyota one-ton truck. This truck is special because it reminds her of horses, her horses, back on the ranch that she runs in her spare time, the place where her heart lies.

For her, the choice of a vehicle parallels the choice of her career and her adaptive management style. Trained as a nutritionist with dreams of becoming an exercise physiologist, she became a technical writer because it was available at a time when she wanted to work, despite the fact that she would have preferred to have continued her education in exercise physiology. She sacrificed for her husband, the man who is also responsible for trading in the car she really loved for the one she now has to drive.

At work she is friendly, efficient, and well respected, known as the only woman to ever win a major argument with a vice-president in the home office, known also as a woman who gets what she wants by combining good looks, charm, and humor with a strong goal orientation. Hers is an adaptive style that takes into account the contingencies of the situation, and an appreciation of the value her employees place on their personal lives.

The third red vehicle in the parking lot is the little Fiat roadster owned by a man in Training who bought it cheap from a former Auburn engineer who didn't know a bad engine from a carburetor adjustment. The Fiat and its owner are rakish individuals, appreciated for their technical prowess but widely regarded as a risky investment. For the owner image is important, although the symbols that make up the image may be only superficial. For example, after buying the car the owner had it painted with screaming red Imron, redid the interior, and added shiny new wheels. Underneath the skin there remains the same basic mechanical condition that worried the original owner. Should he have worried? How much should any of us worry when confronted with a beautiful shell? Particularly one that draws attention to itself, does not fit in with the rest of the culture?

This is where the red cars end, unless you count the muted near-reds, orangy-browns, or faded burgundies that suggest an indecisive character, or the cinnamon Buick owned by the boss, a car that always seems to be surrounded by white Accords, blue Starlets, or bronze Celebrities. But that's going too far, far too far with the cars and their colorful meanings. And having been induced to dwell on the red cars maybe I have stumbled onto the merely symbolic exceptions instead of the symbolic rules: After all, without the intent to connect the way people reflect the values of their cars, it is just a parking lot.

THE FRONT DOOR AND ALL IT SUGGESTS

From the parking lot you enter the building, which is one of those ordinary beige boxes with a pillared facade that suggests anything the sign on the door wants it to suggest, and you see two more significant symbols.

The first is the company logo, which consists only of its name—B-BCSC—interesting because when undisguised it includes the names of the founders (as in Smith & Jones) and because one of them—let's say Smith—left the company over a year ago and for a long time everyone thought the company would become "& Jones" but it didn't, and because the founder who remained behind to run the company, a man fond of using lyrics from Dire Straits to explain company policies, a man who jogs every day and drives a silver Porsche 928, is not the kind of regular Joe you would expect to hang something as simple as his last name on a high-tech computer software company whose major product is "Z-Two." But he did.

This is also the man—let's call him Elliot Jones—who walked into the office one day in blue jeans and inspired a revolution. The blue jeans, he said, were his way of rewarding himself for a hard week of work. In corporate America, it is the simple slogans that seem to move the soul, and so it was with this statement. The idea was that B-BCSC pays its employees every two weeks, and paydays should be special, so why not have a company policy that encourages wearing blue jeans to the office on payday?

The policy went into effect immediately and received the sort of tentative, let-me-see-yours-before-you-see-mine kind of reception that one might expect from a radical shift of tradition. Clothes, after all, are coverings of our personalities as much as our bodies, and the sight of a moderately overweight middle-aged man who sits at a desk for a living wearing Calvins is not necessarily inspiring. Such a man might, if pressed as one senior executive in Huntsville was pressed, buy what amounted to his first-ever pair of blue jeans, not the soft, prewashed kind, but the superstiff starched variety, and, not knowing any better, turn them up at the cuffs and snap them into place with red suspenders, giving all the world and particularly the customers the impression of a farmer on first Saturday at the county fair.

It was not the costume but the calculated effects of the costume on the customers that prompted the strongest criticism. Salespeople in Alabama and Georgia objected to looking too much like where they came from, especially when talking business to someone from San Francisco or Boston. One person in the company took offense to the policy this way: "I'm an adult and I don't need to be told what to wear." However, as the weeks passed Elliot Jones relented a bit in deference to his sales force and modified the policy to encourage "those individuals who did not deal directly with customers" on paydays to wear blue jeans, etc. The revolution was well underway, and its later influences on the culture could not yet be imagined.

The second significant symbol on the door of the Huntsville office of B-BCSC is the sublogo "ZZ" and the fine print beside it: "A company of the ZZ Corporation." This is significant for everyone who draws a pay-check because ZZ—a prestigious but stone-faced firm—could drop this B-BCSC at the end of the current year if profits aren't in harmony with corporation projections.

This symbol also reflects the conscious image building apparent in this culture for the past year or so. During this time certain strategic efforts were made to improve the company's operation, which included a major corporate reorganization under the heading "Alien Spaceships" and the institution of "theme parties" to reward employees for their work efforts. Both of these innovations seriously altered the culture of the corporation: the redesign by the advent of a "savior" and the reorganization of work groups and information flows; the theme parties by the emphasis on unifying appearances in a way that made more complex the levels of interaction among the employees and made more visible the values deeply embedded within the culture.

Before we pass the ZZ symbol and enter the building proper, understand-ing already that the symbol itself stands for far more than it suggests, there is this issue of the "savior" that needs to be understood.

Remember that B-BCSC is undergoing a period of transition, a period of transition from an old management derived from the old local company first called XXX and then, when the world turned futuristic, Megatron, an old management roundly blamed for the current state of affairs, to a new image of itself as the leader of the financial and human-resources software market. Weick poses the problem well when he writes that we need to think of managers as evangelists; and in this case his argument holds substantial merit. The evangelist, like a savior, is an inspirational leader capable of articulating the values of the audience, using them as warrants for new arguments about how things will be. The evangelist, like a savior, also stands apart from the flock, is perceived as different, as special, as being in touch with something or someone greater than the rest.

Henry Peppertree is such an evangelist, the new vice- president of the HR (Human Resources) Business Unit, a man who rose from the mainstream streets of Atlanta last November to save this product division, a basically quiet man with an accounting degree from Tennessee. He is a strong-bodied, attractive male of medium height and thinning blond hair who, at thirty-eight, with a background and value system firmly grounded in sales, looks like the sort of fellow who would consider removing a tie on vacation to be the outer limits of eccentricity, the sort of fellow who is strangely in touch with something or someone greater than the rest of us.

He chose to begin his tenure in Huntsville with a sermon that promised the accomplishment of his mission after one sizzling week of complete corporate hell. This is important for two reasons. It is important because Henry Peppertree as an evangelist has carefully developed his presentational speaking abilities. And second, it is important because the first words he spoke were nonevangelical: "In my previous job I was known as an asshole. And as a son-of-a-bitch. And they were right." He went on to personally reorganize the office beginning that afternoon.

For the remainder of his first week on the job, he moved, promoted, cut, and juggled persons, places, and things. When he found out, through the grapevine, that some individuals were actively seeking employment elsewhere, he issued a company policy against it, saying, in effect, that if he found out about it he would fire that person on the spot, without recommendations, effectively condemning him or her to a long, gray life in corporate limbo. He added, gently, that he was hurt by this lack of loyalty and that if someone was truly dissatisfied, she or he should come in and feel free to talk with him personally about it.

This is also the man who, prior to wandering in the corporate sales desert that was his life before joining B-BCSC, used to run a small restaurant with his father in Huntsville, a barbecue place the B-BCSC people (before B-BCSC was B-BCSC and while it was still XXX and before it was Megatron) came for lunch, a coincidence that reminds people here how small the world actually is, and how strange are its twists of fate. The man who now determines their collective futures was, only a few quick years ago, the same man who took their orders for smoked pig and a couple of bags of green onion chips. In fact, Henry recalls those days often, with pride and in public, and makes it plain that one of his current managers was the reason why the business could turn a profit, his appetite being surpassed only by his girth.

Henry Peppertree's personal evangelical style and humble but mythical past became singularly important in the all-new B-BCSC. He came in hard and made few compromises. He promised that if the product division accomplished his goals, believed in his message, and accepted his ways, that everyone would be rewarded. And then he did one remarkable thing: he challenged the entire customer support department to answer every call and complaint within a six-week span of time (which, given its history, would have been nearly impossible) and said that if they met that deadline he would personally cook a steak dinner for every one of them.

This is the way a corporate culture begins: with an evangelical bang, and then a challenge, and then a dinner.

BEING RECEIVED

Turn right at the front door and you are greeted by the receptionist.

She is always a she and she is always as pretty as she is polite. There is a large sign on her window that says all guests must sign in with her, and the place for your signature was a discarded wedding reception book that asked for not only your name, but your address and your relationship to the bride. It was replaced by a more suitable book that requires your name, the time you registered, the person you were planning to see, and the time you departed the building.

The reception-book changeover corresponds to the advent of Henry and his suspicion that corporate spies could have easy access to the building unless they were carefully monitored. For a while all of the spaces on the reception book were treated seriously, but as the employees, their spouses, the various delivery persons, and other "guests" learned that Mr. Peppertree preferred to be called "Henry" and that some policies could be gotten around creatively enough to make the effort worthwhile, the "careful monitoring" apparently slackened a good bit. For example:

Joe Blow	11 or so	looking for one good woman with whom to share lunch and sexual favors . . .
Large Bear	12:01	To see smaller Bear. No Bear there; No honey either.
Dr. Strangelove	Zero Hour	Desperately seeking Susan

Humor in the receptionist's book is one of several humor motifs that emerge from the culture of B-BCSC. Back in the Training Department one of Gary Larson's calendars hangs over the coffee machine. Employees vote for "Best Cartoon of the Week" and the winner is displayed during the following week, complete with penciled-in comments that often reflect ongoing corporate concerns. One of the finer examples is the well-known Larson cartoon of the hunter's eyepiece focusing on two bears in the woods, in which one bear is pointing toward the other bear as the better target. This cartoon was labeled thusly: hunter = Henry; bear pointing to other bear = name of person who had been promoted to management level; innocent bear = name of person who quit when Henry came aboard.

The receptionist position is one that was subject to high turnover, not because the sign-in book is fouled with humor or because the various women that fulfilled that role lost their looks or forgot their manners, but because in the old culture the belief was that receptionists should look for other, better-paid openings in the company. So at B-BCSC the receptionist was always treated with respect and candor, particularly by spouses of employees who quickly learned that the receptionist today might be their spouse's colleague tomorrow.

This too changed with the advent of Henry. The current receptionist— who, like everyone since the advent of Henry, goes only by first name— is Suzi. She is pretty and polite and possesses a fine sense of humor as well as what is widely regarded to be the best telephone voice in the business. She too is treated with respect and candor, despite the fact that she openly professes no professional aspirations above her current station in the company. This is as it should be, according to Henry, who believes in the value of continuity, particularly continuities of appearances, particularly continuities of appearances among employees of a company in transition.

Suzi is an apostle true to her mission. When you enter the building she greets you, usually by name, and before you have a chance to bypass the book of signing in, she offers to page the person you want to speak to. The goal of her receptionist's rhetoric is control: control of the workspace for which she is responsible, control of the people that walk through the door, and control of the situation that occurs when someone who walks through the door enters her workspace. It is a rhetoric of personal appeal, of logical inducements, designed to reduce the natural ambiguities of the situation.

Once you have been received, if you prefer not to have someone paged and if you give even a marginal appearance of signing in, you may proceed into the body of the building.

WALKING THROUGH THE BUILDING

As you leave the receptionist's area, you move through a maze of adjoining corridors, temporary walls, and meaningful symbols.

The building has a closed-in atmosphere that is made unnerving by the generally cramped quarters, but is made more bearable by the presence of interesting, colorful artifacts. The problem of space was created when the staff expanded beyond the capacities of the building, a problem many of the employees believe will be solved next January when the new building is completed and everyone moves in.

The new building was designed by an Auburn University architecture graduate, a 6'8" former basketball star named JIM (he says it in a way that can only mean all capitals) who cultivated an appreciation for aesthetics, probably from breathing the higher air that he moves around in. He told me that the new B-BCSC building will be "great for Huntsville," which meant that its design was about four years behind Atlanta. It will be two stories of pseudoglass, which is a plastic surface that has the image of the more expensive real thing without the cost or the insulating value. One feature of the new building will be a large white arch over the front door which will give the building the look of a modern church, a feature, according to JIM, that is symbolically rich and absolutely appropriate to Huntsville's native, mostly Baptist, business environment. The office space will be open, with small partitions for the individual workspaces, on the Japanese model. Only the managers will have American-style offices, with doors that close, and walls, and real windows.

The space problem will be solved, but perhaps another problem, a problem more deeply connected to this corporation's culture, will be created. Given the description of the openness and lack of walls in the new structure, where will the colorful posters, the hunk calendars, the tacked-up photographs and plaques, and so forth be displayed? How will these vitally important cultural artifacts survive? And if they do not survive, how will this lack of visual stimuli affect the culture?

The new building is not yet completed, and I have not yet explained the importance of these cultural displays. One significant aspect of the B-BCSC culture is nonverbally clear: There is a strong tradition of individualizing one's office area or workspace. So clear is this tradition that certain motifs become apparent. The motifs include some ordinary and expected symbols: symbols of family and families with pets, symbols of academic and professional achievement, symbols of recognition and reward. These are the positive, traditional symbols that you find in American offices from sea to shining sea, symbols that suggest ordinary values, or, if looked at differently, symbols that suggest exceptional continuities.

A second motif concerns symbols that are inner pathways to a mind-scape of petty fears, rages, senses of humor, and bellicose warnings that coalesce into a collage of general and specific corporate psyches and that oddly enough correspond to the individual positive symbols of home, learning, and achievement.

For example, "Shit Happens" is an emblem, a sort of badge really, that is laced through the building next to degrees and family snapshots, a common source of strategically ambiguous identification with an anonymous but ever-present enemy. "Is This Fun?" and "Are We Having Fun Yet?" also permeate the nonverbal atmosphere, particularly at eye level. The urge for self-preservation and recognition can be seen in the variety of "Me" buttons that tell their own stories: "God, I'm Good!" "Me First," "I'm Wonderful in Bed" "I'm Getting over This," and "I'm Not Crazy" are some examples.

Similarly, identifications with cartoon animals or generally cute things also contribute to the psychological population of B-BCSC: there were, on one count, 14 Garfields, 6 Georgia Bulldogs, 22 Auburn War Eagles, about 15 bears (although some may be mutant raccoons or just fuzzy dogs with no tails), 3 owls, 3 tigers, 4 Nittany Lions, 16 kittens or cats, 8 Snoopies, 2 Shoes, 2 badgers, 2 beavers, and 1 long snake. If you include sports heroes (which is only fair, given that some of the animals represent team affiliations), you have an almost even balance between Pat Dye and Bear Bryant mugs, none of Ray Perkins, and a poster of the Olympic team. If you include male hunks you see evidence for the popularity of Tom Selleck, Tom Cruise, the Miami Vice guys, some nostalgia for Humphrey Bogart and John Wayne, an occasional husband or boyfriend who obviously works out, and—although this one is probably political rather than physical—Ronald Reagan.

A third motif suggests identification with things corporate, such as "Users Conference" posters, memorabilia from company picnics, Christmas parties, and the like. One characteristic of this motif is the absence of symbols drawn from previous places of employment, despite the fact that virtually everyone at B-BCSC held at least one job somewhere else prior to joining the B-BCSC team. This characteristic is easily understood as a show of corporate loyalty or as the nonverbal desire to make blank the past, but it is singularly at odds with other nonverbal symbols that strongly suggest a pride in past associations, schools, achievements, and times. It is also at odds with the talk exchanged among employees in which stories of past companies are routine. Perhaps this means that we guard our nonverbal communication more carefully than our verbal communication, or perhaps it is a broader reflection of a cultural value: To fit in means to make an opening in the symbols of one's life, an opening that represents a space reserved for the present, a space dominated by the visual channels of thought, where how we see or need to be seen can play a major role in demonstrating how we choose to fit in.

But I am getting ahead of my story.

THE OPENING OF A CULTURE

Henry Peppertree promised that he would cook steaks for everyone if the customer support group answered all of its calls and complaints. As the deadline arrived and the challenge had been met, the promise made became the promise kept.

However, this event was more than the bestowing of a reward. It was the first public gathering of the company since the advent of Henry. An opening had been created.

A culture is a sensual experience. It has a look, a feel, a smell, a characteristic way about it. To participate in a culture is to become a motif in support of its general theme, a cog in the corporate wheel, a member of a group. Similarly, to actively create a culture, or to modify or change an existing one, requires the articulation of a theme that unifies disparate elements within an organization. The selection of the theme is an act of rhetorical redefinition, and it offers the choice of identification or division.

The urgency to make the great steak cook-out successful soon became a major effort that actually interfered with work, including the work that had prompted the cook-out.

In this land of nonverbal enchantments, a safe place for blue jeans on paydays, of visual displays that encouraged personalizing the workspace, a new message appeared whose purpose was to acculturate. This message included posters, memos, and hand-drawn invitations that featured a Western theme: Henry's Cook-Out. The posters consisted of likenesses of Henry and his managers dressed in cowboy outfits tending a grill upon which sizzled huge portions of meat. The posters were a sort of corporate invitation that suggested a loosening of the reins, a time to trade in the costumes of seriousness for the costumes of play.

A team was put together to manage the event. The idea of a cook-out, with a Western theme, was supported with a series of other nonverbal inducements. In a revolution that began with a policy concerning blue jeans, it did not seem extraordinary to ask employees to dress Western or to encourage members of the company who owned horses to contribute bales of hay and other ranch items to the training center room, which was decorated for the event. There was a new air of excitement, a sense of common purpose, that integrated work and reward in a way that met the display needs demonstrated by members of this culture.

Talk within the organization centered on the cook-out as an activity that required an effort at fitting in which included what to wear, how to dance, what to do if you didn't eat meat. For a rare few who saw the event as a foolish exercise, as nothing more than an excuse to get a free meal out of the boss, or as a waste of time, this attempt at rhetorical redefinition was decidedly divisive.

Two responses were formed that may be instructive. The first was to mimic the old psychological adage, "I'd rather be sick than stupid." This rhetorical reponse is derived from a widely accepted educational premise: If I'm sick, I don't have to go to school. Furthermore, since the sickness is "beyond my control," I cannot be held accountable for my absence. The second response was the restoration of psychological equity. In this scenario, the premise was articulated this way: "Sure, I'll go. I'll eat his steak, I'll drink his beer, I'll take the afternoon off with pay, and then I'll go out and piss on his tires in the parking lot." Notice the association of the event with the boss, natural enough because it occurred at his suggestion, but odd if you consider the total corporate effort that was required to support it. However, if all that is suggested by that statement is all that is necessary to restore psychological equity to a situation—to start with a clean slate on the next working day—then a free dinner and the minor embarrassment of soiled tires, which would probably be attributed by the owner to a stray dog anyway, is a small price to pay.

One characteristic of the cook-out that separates it from other company-sponsored attempts at a good time—such as the annual picnic or Christmas party—was the decision to exclude spouses and other family members from participation. The idea was explained to me this way: "Get the people together who work together and let them have a good time. You know what happens when everybody's wife or husband comes—you spend your time with them. This party was for us." As a strategy for building a culture, this decision further suggests the need to amplify the commonly shared sense of community that separates the public from the private life. It also was

cheaper, if you take into account the cost of the steaks, but that consideration did not figure prominently in the discussions about it.

For those who chose to attend, which was the vast majority, the event
was culturally significant. The steaks were perfect, the liquor was cheap
but free, and the music was as playful as the dancers could be. People
enjoyed themselves, had fun as a culture, and learned to see Henry as
a person whose dour corporate countenance was complemented by a
demonstration of his desire not only to redefine, but to fit in. Things
loosened up at B-BCSC a good bit after that, but not by sacrificing the
goals or the quality of effort required to attain them. It was more akin
to a regional office's rite of passage, an initiation to a new sense of itself
rooted in the articulated value that marked the short speech given by
Henry before the event started: "If we all work hard, then we can play
hard too."

In our culture, when you change clothes you can become a different
person.

When you agree to wear a costume, you agree to participate in a
cultural standard, demonstrate nonverbally your willingness to fit in.
People eat steaks every day wearing suits and ties or fashionable skirts.
To suggest to a group of working adults that they need to step out of
their ordinary costumes and into a sort of fantasy, a fantasy that is at
least one or two steps down from the ordinary level of costuming, is to
further suggest that they can loosen up, and perhaps by so loosening,
they can become different. But different in this sense means closer to the
heart, more real, more honest, able to talk more freely, another example
of the odd connection between nonverbal displays and the choice of
verbal style. Over time, would this quarterly changing of clothes lead to
improved understandings? Would the idea of costume parties, an idea
that seems to be naturally drawn from the nonverbal display value of the
culture of B-BCSC, lead to a greater sense of shared community? How
would this motif support the emergence of a common cultural theme?

THE MAKING OF A RITUAL IN CELEBRATION'S CLOTHES

The next decision concerning clothing came soon after the cook-
out, when Henry decided to throw another party.

This time it was decided the party would be a '50s bash, complete with a disc jockey, turning the training center into a replica of a high-school gym and featuring a menu that included burgers and dogs, cokes and beer. Again the halls were decked out in posters inviting participation in the party with the warning "No one allowed in without bobby sox."

The theme to have a theme, a theme with costumes and music, a reward larger than wearing blue jeans on paydays, began to surface as an emblem of this culture. From the top down the theme was determined and communicated, and, at least from the point of view at the top, the need to celebrate a product release or the satisfaction of a goal would be dramatized by the enactment of these scenes, the completion of which would mark the company's transcendence to a new level of harmony and efficiency. At the home office, around this same time, Elliot Jones sponsored a beach party that included hauling in two tons of sand that was deposited in the center of corporate headquarters and ordering everyone to appear in bathing suits.

The '50s party inspired a competitive spirit among the managers responsible for planning and coordinating the activities and among the employees for whom the party was intended. This latter point is worth belaboring a little more. One characteristic of the cultural display fostered by B-BCSC is its top-down, hierarchically consummating appearance. Remember it was Elliot Jones who began the blue jeans revolution, and it was Henry Peppertree who ordered these festivities. Furthermore, in Huntsville the managers were put in charge of the events with the goal of "entertaining the employees," those hierarchical inferiors whose role in the display is to observe it passively while being required to imitate the clothes of their superiors. In the home office, however, this is not the case. Their celebrations are total company efforts, and managers are not primarily responsible for bringing off the event. Perhaps this suggests that the more fully evolved culture of the home office displays more integration; the less fully evolved culture of the regional office in Huntsville displays more differentiation, and thus more of a need to delegate and to direct.

The competitive spirit of the managers, a spirit in part to best the previous effort and in part to best each other, soon filtered down to the employees. During this time discussions about costumes, particularly about the truth concerning '50s styles—whether bobby sox or hose should be worn with full party skirts, whether greaser hairdos were actually dominant among young men of the period—were special features of any otherwise task-related discussion. Another notable feature was the fact that some of these discussions occurred behind closed doors—rare at B-BCSC—leading to widespread speculation about what was being plotted. Was it true that Angela's group was actually taking roller-skating lessons at night to appear more competent at the bash dressed up as drive-in waitresses on wheels? Was Bob really having a toupee fashioned for the event to look like Elvis? One afternoon I dropped in and found the entire documentation group practicing their dancing while a group in customer education was sweatily engaged in a collective attempt to master the hula hoop. And so it went.

On the day of the party one genuine surprise was the appearance of a vintage 1954 MG-TF in the parking lot.

This car, completely restored just in time to be seen at the event, was a sign of the total effort required to have fun by dedicating your efforts to fitting in. At the party, the managers performed a series of skits with corporate and '50s themes that were analogically correct renditions of current company attitudes and values, and these skits were videotaped for archival purposes. The party was also marked by the presentation of a special award to Henry, who was, I was told, taken completely by surprise by it. He stood up quietly, fumbled for words, looked genuinely touched by the award, explained briefly that he wasn't very good at accepting thanks, thanked them, and then gave a short speech about how well this division was doing which ended when he announced that the next party would be for Halloween.

The '50s party was apparently an exhausting success. As a further loosening of the culture it was accompanied by some memorable groping, a few incidences of the old slap-and-tickle routines, and the usual drinking to excess on the part of a few excessively red-faced males. Although these sorts of violations of ordinary working relationships are fairly common in American organizations, they were clearly uncommon at B-BCSC. So uncommon, in fact, that on the following Monday morning, at the weekly management meeting, there was some serious soul-searching and a recommendation that drinking be limited, somehow. It was rumored that a couple of marriages might be in jeopardy if this sort of thing continued, and that perhaps it might be wise to invite the spouses to future events. This recommendation was considered, but it was not acted upon. There seemed to be the feeling that these company events should continue to be limited to company employees, that the whole thing might change for the worse if foreigners were allowed to witness what the natives actually did.

If the looseness displayed by a culture when it is encouraged to be loose becomes a source of its identity, its way of knowing about itself, then it also becomes a boundary, an invisible but commonly understood limit marking, as if by some unspoken common decree, its collective emotions, the moments of its community, the material of its own mythologies. When a culture is being built, the players are living through those myths, experiencing those emotions, evolving their community. In this way their decision to limit the intrusions of outsiders can be understood and perhaps appreciated. They are having the fun of doing, which is always secretly more exciting than just having it to begin with.

A culture that can be made, fashioned in one's own image, complete with myths and legends that you are a part of, with costumes that you wore and stories told and retold that you play a leading part in, is a powerful inducement to limit who can play in this small but vivid drama of modern corporate life. It is the costumes that created the opportunities, the clothes that signified the need to reach out for some universal meaning, for some image that could unify at first just the appearances, but later the realities of this particular sense of place. The clothes were fantasies, fantasies that you could put on and pretend in, and what was pretended in them was open to free associations and the working out analogically of perceptual disparities, a chance to creatively enact a common theme. Taken as a form of cultural experience, compared to similar rituals drawn from the broader spectrum of American life, it would seem that these theme parties were a vital source of organizational therapy that this culture in transition needed to go through.

THOSE WHO DON'T PLAY, WHO DON'T FIT IN, OR WHO ARE JUST STRANGE

Every culture has a way of dealing with its misfits.

In our time, and in our land, these unfortunates are labeled as being crazy, with an endless variety of causes for being and ways to be that way. The usual treatment for someone judged crazy is therapy, and every known therapy exhibits some form of a scapegoat.

If building an organization's culture can be viewed as an attempt to unify its values as well as its appearances and behaviors, then it can also be said that culture building is a practical form of organizational therapy. So it would seem plausible that within such an organization crazies would exist and that attempts would be made to profane and to purify them. Such is my assessment of the particular case of B-BCSC.

In America we have learned how to say the word "schizophrenia." Although schizophrenia is typically more complex than the mere exhibition of dual or multiple personalities, in the language of the the workplace "schizophrenia" covers a wide range of maladies from mood changes to full-blown, baying-at-the-moon-madness. This is easily understood when you consider that the informal evaluation of craziness often means little more than that person is different from us. Because all of us walk around believing we are right at least most of the time, there is good reason to suspect that everyone else is potentially crazy.

At B-BCSC there are two kinds of schizophrenics. The first is, by the odd logic of a diversified society that we have grown accustomed to, actually "normal," in the sense that most of us are necessarily two or more people most of the time. Symptoms of this form of the disease are the belief that we "really are" or at least deserve to be someone else, combined with the articulation of those beliefs to others who accept them as more or less valid. It is normal because it is accepted, and it is accepted because its meaning is widely shared.

For example, boom-generation individuals were reared on the affluent middle-class belief in their own personal worth, a worth that should culminate in a self-actualizing life. It is therefore not uncommon to find individuals who work at one job to make a living, but who "believe" they are destined for some other existence, generally more romantic and financially profitable. Recall the woman who owns the red Renault, a person who works at B-BCSC but is at home an artist. Recall the woman who owns the red Jetta, a person who works at B-BCSC but lives another life managing a small horse ranch. In the home office there is a manager who edits a poetry journal, and in Huntsville there is an individual who keeps a diary of everything that happens to her at work—notes, says she, for a novel she is planning to write.

If these examples strike us as the rule more than the exception, it is perhaps because we can identify closely with them. Within the organization, where routine talk is exchanged that weaves the private with the public, the persona we speak out of is necessarily complex. At B-BCSC those personae become part of the conversational rules about appropriateness, rules that include a casual acceptance of the secret lives revealed in them, rules that suggest that if an individual has no such secrets or is unwilling or unable to talk about them, then he or she is perhaps a little bit strange. To fit in at B-BCSC is to be more than one person, and to succeed within the culture may require acceptable choices of alternative personae.

The second form of schizophrenia is less common, far less positive, and thus far more likely to stand out as an appearance notable for its uniqueness. It is marked by the presence of a communicative style that wanders over the border of the real in persistent and culturally unacceptable ways. For example, one woman was described to me as "crazy" because "she will tell you what she did last night and then turn around the next minute and tell you something different." The general attribution given to this behavior is the excessive desire to "fit in," to find something to say to become part of a conversation despite the lack of truth behind what is said. The alternative persona must be consistent if it is not to be judged crazy. Because this woman is, as another person put it, "either very smart or just knows all the words" and is technically competent at her job, she is tolerated within the culture. In some cases, as R. D. Laing pointed out twenty years ago, a schizophrenic personality is forgiven if the resulting craziness is found to be creative or valuable to the culture.

However, the case of this woman is made more interesting because she is also regularly blamed for events that are clearly beyond her control. In one case she was assumed to be the cause for a man leaving the company, a man she had, the story goes, consummated an affair with. Affairs between consenting adults is not unusual in a corporate culture, but this one so tainted the image of the individuals involved as to dramatically affect how others treated them. And so, the story goes, the man left the company, and it was all the woman's fault.

This example goes beyond simple chauvinism, despite the fact that it was women who blamed the woman. It places the woman in the position of a scapegoat, a person who takes the flak, as Bonnie Johnson used to say, for anything that goes wrong. In this case, the man left the company at least in part because he received a serious salary boost to join another firm and because he had been passed over for promotion to a managerial rank at B-BCSC for reasons that had little if anything to do with his sexual behavior.

Another widely retold episode of this woman's craziness occurred prior to the '50s party. Like everyone else, she was at least partially consumed by a desire to dress for success on this particularly important cultural occasion. When she showed up she was surprised to find out that her costume was "all wrong" and required the total efforts of her work group to make it "right." Her acquiescence to being physically redressed signaled her need to fit in, her desire to do what was necessary to win approval from her peers; however, from the other side of it the drama also suggests the need of the peers to use the scapegoat as a projection of their own fears about inadequacy. By releasing their pent-up emotions on someone whose only crime was to look "a little more sixty-ish than fifty-ish" for a corporate good time, there seems to be more to this story of a costume than what can possibly meet the eye.

You may be wondering, as I did, why this woman, who obviously does not fit into the evolving mainstream of this company's culture, has not been fired. It is true that she must know by now how the culture feels about her. If she hasn't been fired, then why hasn't she left of her own accord? I would argue that it is essential to this organization's culture, particularly one in the therapeutic stages I have described, to maintain a scapegoat or two. What better way exists to maintain equilibrium in times of stress? And I would also argue that perhaps she has not chosen to abandon this culture because in her own way she understands exactly how she fits in and is willing to accept it, something like a shunned Amish person who is happy enough to exist on the fringes of his or her chosen society.

The organizational scapegoat may be necessary to a company that derives its rules from its exceptions, its ways of knowing and being and doing from a commonly accepted standard for the interdependence of integration and differentiation. Without them, the members of the organization would have to blame themselves, and their own mistakes, for the feelings they cannot abide. With a scapegoat on board, life is easier because there is always someone there who is worse off than you. For a company in a period of transition, a time marked by constant stress and strain, marked also by the desire to build a culture in which it is possible to know what fits, the scapegoat serves the best interests of the organization.

Perhaps this is a characteristic of most hierarchically driven organizations, but I doubt it. Instead, I think it is probably a vital part of an organization in cultural transition, an organization that is creating its own legends and myths in the stories it tells about itself; after all, some of those stories need the jazz, the craziness, the perceived weirdness of those who violate the culture. The exception may legitimize the rule.

GOING OUT

It is hard to say good-bye to Suzi on the way out.

Her job is beginnings, not endings, and besides, she always seems to be busy. If you think about it, she probably has a hard time with endings, given her lack of practice. On the telephone she greets and pages, plugs in whatever she plugs in to connect you to who or what you have asked for. When you have completed your conversation, you hang up. The switchboard operator, in this case the receptionist, never gets a chance to say goodbye.

But perhaps this too is as it should be for this culture. When you leave B-BCSC nothing is ever completely over. If you are an employee, there is always tomorrow and the work it brings. If you are a visitor, chances are good you will be back. And if you are an investigator of an organization's culture, leaving the place you came into with questions means leaving without all the answers you need. A culture in transition is not a very stable place.

This is the place in the story reserved for summary impressions.

Because I have already put them into words, and this essay is longer than I intended, I will instead discuss some of what I observed and interpreted but did not already include. Call them interpretive regrets, I guess.

On the verbal aspects of this culture I regret quite a bit. I regret not doing some of what I intended to do, such as explaining the communicative functions of the story-swap, or exploring corporate giveaways at Christmas parties and picnics, like the pig hat awarded to the male chauvinist of the year who really was one but was somehow changed by the experience, or the time Henry called a company meeting to give an on-the-spot bonus check to two men who had worked serious overtime to get the job done, both of them rendered speechless by the situation. Nor did I get a proper shot at explaining why it is that so many employees keep a radio on in their offices even though they seldom listen to it, which is a fact I personally attribute to a need for background against which to act out their dramas. Nor did I discuss the flows of information and the networks they spawn, which I spent better than two months of my life charting, a fact I personally attribute to my fear that empirical reality might actually mean something even though for me it usually doesn't, and in the case of B-BCSC, it really didn't.

On the nonverbal side of the culture I regret not including a section on the symbolism of the "Hey Elliot!" and "Hey B-BCSC!" instant memo sheets that guarantee a quick and honest flow of information and suggestions between the founder and his flock. Nor did I spend any time on the nonverbal differences between the home office, with its rich and expensive textures, its lines of leased executive Mercedes, Porsches, Audis, and Corvettes, and the plainer, less ostentatous ornaments of the regional office in Huntsville.

Nor did I—and this is the part of the whole thing that really bothers me—find out what the theme of the B-BCSC culture is. If I were more of a Christian I might have seen the advent of the savior as some sort of Jesus Christ equivalent played out in the regional offices of a Nazareth called Huntsville, and found lessons in his speeches, and looked around for jealous Romans. But it wasn't the same.

If I were more of a trash sociologist I might have emptied garbage and found some code in the leftover containers of yogurt, the wrappers from microwave dinners that feature a calorically sensitive motif, or the doodles of dreamers who scribble things that look like bank account balances in the upper-left-hand corners of memos concerning the delay of automatic deposits due to changeover in the computer system. But I only did a little bit of that and it didn't add up to much.

Once, though, in a cocktail conversation with the company programming genius, I might have gotten it. He told me what more and more looks to me like the theme based on his own understanding of what Z-Two looked like, as a concept. As he told it to me—and I should point out that he is the only person in the entire organization who actually knows what makes the system work because nobody has ever been able to draw it, document it, or otherwise get it down on paper—a certain something happened to him. It was in his eyes, I think, the way they squinted as if seeing something clearly that had recently, perhaps painfully, been forgotten until just now, but I might be wrong about that. Anyway, this is what he told me, and if it looks like a poem it's because he said it that way:

> The beauty of the thing is how it changes,
> to accommodate new information,
> to become the environment,

to meet the total needs of the user.
It looks like a three-dimensional spider's web,
all of that mysterious calculus,
all of those prize soft numbers.
I don't know.
I made it,
and I don't even know all
of what it is.

Back in the parking lot I remember that this is the guy who drives the Prelude. How appropriate for an evolving product in a transitional office. No, it isn't just appropriate, it's perfect. Maybe it is the theme . . .

3

The Way the World Ends:
Inside Star Wars

Percentage change since 1981 in the amount the Pentagon spends on classified projects: +300

Percentage of the funds the Pentagon has requested since 1981 that Congress has appropriated: 92.1

Percentage of new government R&D spending that went to Star Wars in 1986: 22

Percentage increase since 1980 in political contributions by the top 20 defense contractors: 100

Number of the top six military contractors that have paid less than 3 percent in federal income taxes annually since 1981: 5

Number of U.S. Air Force personnel assigned to investigations and counterintelligence: 1,423

Number assigned to public affairs: 1,862

Number of U.S. university scientists who have pledged to refuse Star Wars research funds: 3,800

Percentage of Americans who think science and technology may destroy the human race: 74

Percentage who believe Heaven exists: 84

Percentage who expect to enter therein: 66

Percentage who think the afterlife will be boring: 5

Percentage of Soviet children who believe a nuclear war can be prevented: 92

Percentage of American children who believe this: 65

—*The Harper's Index*

One day you read in the newspaper that General Eugene Fox has assumed command of the Strategic Defense Initiative in Huntsville.

How appropriate, you muse. A fox is known to be a creature of superior cunning and skill. And you think nothing more about it.

No jets fly overhead, either.

Days pass as days do pass, like wind through trees, gusts following breezes following what seems to be long, quiet periods of calm. More news about Star Wars appears in the papers but you think nothing much of it.

On the way to work one morning you consider what sort of organizational culture the Star Wars Command engenders. But you let it pass.

One of your students works there and you mention it to him as a research opportunity for a term paper. He is enthusiastic. You pay it no more attention than you do any other term-paper topic. It is a matter of convenience for him, a small thing.

In the national newspapers and on National Public Radio there seems to be increasing debate about Star Wars. Unions of concerned scientists form, make rhetoric, disagree among themselves. Locally there is no news like this. You think nothing of it.

Ten weeks pass. The student turns in his term paper and the title "Lost in Space" amuses you. You read it on your own back porch late in the afternoon, late in summer. It is not amusing. The student has juxtaposed scenes taken directly from the Star Wars television series with daily life in the real Planet Earth Star Wars Command.

But the real life isn't anything like the fiction.

He tells of unspeakable plans, unnatural contracts, and one room in which all the doom is played out. He says, of course, that none of this is true, he has changed the names to protect the innocent, etc. He does, however, require that you share it with no one and return it to him after it is graded.

The paper ends with the world going out of business in 1993.

This is 1987.

At a party you are standing with a group of Star Wars contractors and the common talk is Star Wars contracts.

At first there is the usual gung ho, beat-the-Russians sort of thing. But you notice that it winds down pretty quickly and uneasy looks are passed around.

"We may be in over our heads," one guy says, sadly.

Throats are cleared, shoulders are grabbed onto and for once honest eyes are everywhere.

"Somebody's got to do it," somebody says.

That's it.

Somebody indeed.

You attend the annual Mooreland Hunt Ball and your wife is in her element. This has been the season of the fox seen, but not caught. There is a big band doing big band tunes, everyone who is anyone in Huntsville is decked out in expensive attire and dancing.

You prefer to stand with a bourbon on the edge of the crowd, looking for clues.

You are introduced to a military officer and casually ask him what he does.

"I teach the tactical and strategic uses of nuclear weapons," he responds.

"Really?"

He nods. "It's great! A lot of fun."

"How did you get into this line of work?"

"I got drafted back in 1971. One thing led into another and I developed this specialty."

"Do you like it?"

He looks at me for a while before answering. "Yes," he says. "I like it a lot."

"How do you do it?"

"Do what?"

"Teach the tactical and strategic uses of nuclear weapons?"

He perks up a bit as ours has become the topic of the table. "Well, it's a big game, really. You choose up sides and blow each other up until someone wins." He grins.

"What do you think about Star Wars?"

He stops grinning. "What do you mean?"

"I mean do you think it will work?"

"I can't answer that," he says. He quickly turns to his wife and asks her to dance.

You begin to think about how strange it is to live in a town that plans the end of the world. You begin to wonder, seriously, what goes on in a place like that.

Curiosity is like hearing a song on the radio and not being able to figure out the words. It's like constantly hearing the same song and still not being able to figure the words out.

Now if you are an ordinary person the thing to do is go out and buy the record, listen to it, master the words and be done with it. If you are a slightly unordinary person, say an academic, the thing to do is go to the store and read the sheet music and be done with it. But if you are a detective, let's say an organizational detective, and if you are afflicted with curiosity about the words that fit the music, life isn't as easy or as neat.

This is because you see the problem differently. You define it not as an impersonal desire, a simple lust that, for example, can be satisfied either by purchasing the object itself or by studying it in someone else's store. No.

Instead you recognize the problem as something deeper, at once a symbolic convergence of you and it, a process alive with motives, feelings, strategies, meanings. It becomes an interpretive opportunity from which you will learn lessons that you would have perhaps been better off not learning, an experience that will change, possibly forever, your views, your attitudes, your sense of self.

With curiosity comes danger, a little lift out of everyday life. You want to learn the words to a song, that's all? Friend, that isn't even the beginning.

For you have learned how to read. And with knowledge comes obligation.

You begin slowly. You drive past the Strategic Defense Command, 106 Wynn Drive, noticing small, seemingly insignificant details.

The colors of cars.

The presence of a flag.

The position of guards.

You begin to fit them together. You discover that when a certain silver Mazda RX-7 is parked by the entrance a flag with two stars is put out. You notice that when this happens two men in dark sunglasses emerge from the building and begin reconnoitering the parking lot.

Pretending to take a wrong turn you turn into the parking lot and pull into that parking space and a guard comes out. "Sorry, sir," he says, not sure if he should salute you or shoot you, "this space is reserved for the general."

You apologize, ask whether this is the BMD (Ballistic Missile Defense) building, and are given polite directions out of here.

A colleague on the faculty who may or may not still work for the CIA and who is very active in the local peace movement has a file of information on SDI.

Truth is he suspects that *you* work for the Company because your father may have. You know that in many ways it is, in fact, a family-oriented business.

Partly through innuendo and partly through scholarly ambiguity you let on that you are working on a project involving local high-tech organizations that support military operations. In the course of your conversation he tells you he has a file on SDI.

You are, of course, surprised. But you say nothing of it. You wonder, aloud, how this might fit in with your research.

He says it might help.

You agree, somewhat reluctantly, to give a look.

All of this seemingly trivial exchange is carried out with high analogic communication content. You know that he assumes you have access to files that you don't have access to or even know about. You never actually deny it, although you grin and use excessive hand gestures when a hint of it comes up. The more you almost deny it, the more likely it is to be true. *Thou protesteth too much!* Sometimes it is more important to be able to act badly than to act well.

So why would this person go out of his way to help you? If he thinks you know what you know, why doesn't he just say so?

The answer is part of the family business. In intelligence work you never know who your friends are. An informer could be an informant. For all he knows you could be his superior, just checking up on him, seeing if his files are up-to-date.

These are the facts of an uneasy life.

The files are public stuff with some useful time lines, queries in the columns, and so forth.

You return them after making a few xerox copies and tell him they seem to be useful.

He seems relieved.

Nothing else passes between you.

Now you may be wondering why there is all this secretive, covert, sneaky stuff going on.

Why not boldly announce your intentions? Go ye forth and sin no more! After all, you are an academic with the appropriate credentials, a researcher, an interested party.

The answer is this: If you ask them for information, they will tell you what they want you to know. From their point of view you are "the public," and their job is "public relations."

Forget for a moment that this is Star Wars. Select any organization you want to select, explain to yourself the nature of your curiosity about communication, culture, information, and then ask yourself what you need to do. The big word in that sentence is *need,* followed by the verb *to do.*

We aren't talking just academic publication, for which none of this is necessary, and even if it was it probably wouldn't reach print because it lacks endnotes, smacks of rebellion against tradition.

We aren't talking lectures to your students, either. Did Indiana Jones tell his class how he escaped from the ruins? Did he explain his relationship to his rival? It wasn't until wonderful old Malinowski died that his truths came out, and then nobody in academe really wanted to believe them.

We aren't talking theory here, we're talking *research.*

We are talking about the satisfaction of a curiosity.

We are talking about the work of a reading.

We are talking about getting at truth.

You need to make an inside contact.

You consider your options. The news is full of them. Hire a call girl to romance a Marine. You chuck that one because you don't know any call girls and anyway there aren't any Marines at Star Wars, this is an Army operation. You could bribe someone, but not on your salary and besides you don't work for a foreign government. More importantly, these are silly ways to get inside. They are too complicated, too indirect, they involve too many other people.

Most importantly, they aren't honest.

Remember the student who wrote the paper?

You tell him you want to study the culture of the SDI office. You tell him only the truth, no hedging around, no strategic ambiguity, no analogic dances. He isn't your student anymore so he can tell you to go to hell if he wants to.

He doesn't tell you that. He says, "No problem."

He says he can make you a visitor.

He says he can introduce you to some people.

He says you will be surprised.

"This is where the world ends," she says as she slowly opens the door.

We enter a cool, overstuffed room of government grays and greens, a room whose western walls are lined with monitors of the blue planet hard-wired to laser printers nested among tall, torn stacks of computer paper upon which are charted the events of various scenarios of war, a room whose two human inhabitants (there are only ever two inhabitants) are known only by code names, and their names are Adam and Eve.

"This is the simulation room," she continues, tossing her red hair back with a laugh. "Not quite as nifty as in the movies, but far more intense, wouldn't you agree?" I watch a television screen enacting an afternoon theater of a thermonuclear war made out of mathematical probabilities and space physics, fiber optics and prevailing winds, watch as our Homing Overlay Experimental Vehicle intercepts some of Theirs and lets others through, watch as our Terminal Imaging Radar sends kill signals to the High Endoatmospheric Defense Interceptors, but too late by a few nagging nanoseconds, see cities that were once named Chicago, Newark, Dallas, and Cheyenne come to a common digital end: blip, blip, blip, blip.

"Shit!" Adam pounds his fist on the top of a terminal. "We *always* lose!"

Eve turns with the printout and walks quietly from the room.

They won't let me tell you her name, so I will call her Mystery. Nor am I allowed to describe her physical appearance, so I will make her an ageless, redheaded, medium beauty.

Attached to her SDI security clearance, worn just above her heart, is a button that reads "Teach Peace." Below it is another that says "Blood Drive Contributor." Next to her official mugshot on the same card is a kid's sticker of Mr. Yuk, green with an ugly tongue sticking out.

"I never thought I'd end up doing this," she tells me.

There is an open courtyard at the center of the Star Wars Command that probably was once a lush garden and Eve is staring at it. She is eating, and I mean really eating, a perfect red apple.

"No one ever goes in there anymore," she tells me. Her words are brief sibilant whispers, she is dark and her eyes are green.

"Why not?"

She takes a bite of the apple, reflects on it, and just shrugs. "Everyone else can see you."

At every turn in the corridor are two uniformed armed guards, most of whom are brunettes. You are supposed to identify yourself, allow them to inspect your clearance card, not talk much, and then, unless something is wrong and one of them has to kill you, move on.

I am allowed to move on, although not without a certain hesitation, as if my motives are dubious or my patriotism is in doubt.

Mystery is with me but obviously has no clout. "Right now," she says, "in Langley, your entire life is being reviewed. We do that for most of our visitors. If something negative shows up one of the guards will, depending on how bad it is, either arrest you for questioning or shoot you on the spot."

I laugh nervously.

She doesn't.

On the way to the shredder we pass Battle Management and hear nothing, Crisis Management and hear nothing, and Public Relations where the sounds of nothing and laughter coalesce in a constant hum. I notice that no one speaks in the halls, eye contact is minimal and more likely the eyes upon you will search for the numbers and colors of your clearance card.

I am a red/blue seven.

The sign on the cafeteria door is missing a letter. "Microwave in Us," it says.

The sign on every restroom door says "Open Slowly!" with a man's face being smashed by a person who didn't.

On the women's bulletin boards are Equal Opportunity announcements. On the men's bulletin boards there are none. On the bulletin board reserved for personal notices I see that Tennessee walking horses are the favored breed, that "approved" babysitters are in constant demand, and that temporary housing near the Kwajalein Missile Range is now available.

And this:

TAKE TIME OUT TODAY TO VISIT THE ADVANCED CONCEPTS ZOO (2B100). SEE A STARTLING EXAMPLE OF HOW ADVANCED AGE EFFECTS THE HUMAN SPECIES. WHILE YOU'RE THERE, BE SURE TO HUMOR THE EXHIBIT—IT'S _____'S BIRTHDAY!

Suddenly every door seems to close.

There are scars on the walls.

I am not allowed to ask questions, take notes, tape-record anything, or make telephone calls.

A few months ago a New York *Times* reporter came through here with a small portable computer. After every stop on his tour he hooked up a modem to a telephone and transmitted his notes back to his office. As the story goes, he was smug and everyone was friendly.

What he didn't know was that every telephone is tapped and connected to a scrambler. Nothing leaves here uninspected. If he had transmitted anything remotely secret it would have been mysteriously "lost."

Apparently some of it was.

Without evidence there is no argument. Without an argument supported by evidence there is no truth. And with no truth to be gotten at by arguments and supporting evidence, there is only personal opinion, the surmise of biases because known facts can be scrambled by machines in the service of paid experts whose jobs are the real and only substantive issue.

That is why I call this a fiction.

Believe it, or not.

There are more suspected KGB agents in Huntsville, Alabama, than anywhere else in the country, save one place whose name I am not allowed to speak.

Imagine that.

I look for clues in fast-food restaurants, during fill-ups at Amoco, Shell, and Exxon, around the campus I used to believe was only a campus in a town that was only a town. At one of the Arab Gulf stations I notice that the common language is Russian. In the aftermath of an argument about prices with a parts man at the BMW dealership, I see two men inside a Turbo Volvo exchanging words and cash.

I think maybe I am imagining all this.

Then one day I call the State Department for information about Clare Boothe Luce, who was at one time my father's boss, and the woman on the other end says, "Yes, Mr. Goodall, but we thought you were dead."

Maybe she meant my father.

Maybe she didn't.

My wife and I regularly receive phone calls from people who claim to be trying to reach other people.

This used to be a source of humor for us. For example, one elderly lady, probably lonesome and always late at night, regularly dials a "7" instead of a "4" due to what we imagine is poor eyesight and insists on calling me "Mary."

"Ma'am," I reply, "I am a man, not a woman, and my name isn't Mary."

"Oh, Mary," she continues, "don't kid me like that."

Then she hangs up.

Most of the calls are from men who, I believe, are faking Southern accents when they ask for Pete, or Fish, or Jug. I say "faking" because there seems to be little honesty in their voices. When I tell them that nobody by that name lives here, they tell me that can't be so.

This admittedly upsets me.

The two-star flag is out, and the general's silver RX-7 is parked in the space reserved for it. Parking spaces at the Star Wars Command are assigned according to rank, and I learn that Adam drives a mucky red Ford 4x4 and Eve comes to work in a solid white Grand Am.

It is hot and my car is black.

A man in a beige polyester suit and Foster Grants removes a notebook from his pocket and writes down my license number. He stares at me, says nothing.

"Why did you do that?" I ask.

He still says nothing. After what seems like a five-count he walks away.

One ordinary morning a man from the Department of Defense walks into my office and flashes his official ID. Then he closes the door.

He tells me he is conducting a security clearance for a colleague of mine who works summers at NASA.

He asks how long I have known him.

Three years.

He asks whether or not this man has friends who are foreign nationals.

I don't think so. There is a Chinese guy in robotics that he works with, but that's the only one I know about.

He asks me if I know of any trips outside the United States this man has made during the past year.

None that I know of. He did go to Hawaii for a conference, but that's part of the United States.

Just barely, the man says. He forces a smile.

So do I.

Do you think there is any reason to suspect that this man is a threat to the security of the United States?

No.

Are you?

I certainly hope not.

So do we, Dr. Goodall.

I am no longer allowed in the Simulation Room.

Mystery is in D.C.

I am introduced to a battle management analyst in the cafeteria who wants to talk. The man smokes, talks, coughs, smokes. He gives the impression of a thin French existentialist who operates a secret underground resistance. He is a civilian.

"Will SDI work?" I ask him.

"No." He smokes, coughs. "Not at least until the year 2000. The science just isn't there."

"But I heard this morning that early deployment is expected, maybe by 1993."

"Oh, we'll deploy something by then. But it won't work."

I am depressed and confused by this information. It makes me want to smoke, cough, talk.

"Then what is the point of all this?"

He stares at me as if I am the dumbest citizen on earth. "Don't you understand anything? What do you think really happens here?"

I guess I am a dumb citizen and know I am out on a limb.

He draws the letters M-A-J-I-C on the corner of his napkin. "Missiles, Appropriations, Jobs, Illusions, and Contractors. That's the whole thing. The big picture."

I am way out on the dumb limb now.

"This is how it works. For thirty years we have made Missiles, etc. Every advance in technology has a price. Every price has multiple bids. As the technology improves, the price goes up, the bids multiply, more and more people are employed. This means money—3.7 billion this fiscal year, which means Appropriations—way more than that because what we spend here is never on the books, and besides, the books never balance, which all adds up to Jobs." He stops, coughs.

Maybe if it ended there we would be all right. But you have to take into account politics—he points to the "I" in illusions, then moves to the "C" for contractors—which means also taking into account, or should

I say "accounting," the interested parties known locally as contractors. "These are not people who make missiles, but who make careers." He coughs.

"Look around. Every one of these young captains in a green uniform wants to make major or light colonel before his twenty are up. They will walk out of this building on the day they retire and move over into the lucrative local contracting industry. In a week or two they march back into this building wearing sharper suits. They have crossed the bridge to the other side armed with knowledge, experience, and contacts. Now they make more money, so they ask for more money. And guess who they ask?"

I say nothing.

"The people who want to make it to the other side." He lights a new cigarette, coughs awkwardly. "Hell, people still call me colonel and I've been out of the service for fifteen years."

"What do you do here?" I know that's one question I'm not supposed to ask.

"I analyze what the contractors tell us."

"And what do the contractors tell you?"

He smokes, coughs. "That it won't work."

"And what do you do with that information?"

He smiles. "I tell my superiors we need more money."

One of the armed guards, a small brunette in late middle age who I learn was a janitor until two months ago when some affirmative action came down, asks for my driver's license.

I give it to her.

Then she asks for a credit card.

I balk.

She grins. "Just playin' with you, honey."

The other guard, a man, pretends that none of this has happened.

Did you imagine that the heart of the Strategic Defense Initiative would be housed in an old red brick building in Alabama? Or did you think as I did, as the movies, the president, and the television have taught us to think, that all this Star Wars stuff would be somehow grander?

Believe me, this is nothing like what is on television.

Nor is it anything like *War Games*, the movie.

This is dullsville with no dialogue.

This is standard government issue.

Maybe this isn't where, but only the way, the world ends.

There is no T. S. bang, there is no T. S. whimper. Just a few thousand blips gone wrong on a star that knows nothing of this.

I weep for the defense of my country, O God.

Between you and me is not only a rocket trajectory, but also a life. You will come to understand that between the two points, in the five minutes, *it* lives an entire life. You haven't even learned the data on our side of the flight profile, the visible or trackable. Beyond them there's so much more, so much none of us know.

—Thomas Pynchon,
Gravity's Rainbow

4

Lost in Space: The Layers of Illusion Called Adult Space Camp

Reading these pictures in a sentence gives you
one kind of feeling, depending on your experience
and imagination. Seeing them on a movie screen,
animated by flickering light and existing in se-
quential time, can give you a very different feeling, can tell you different things. . . . Thinking
in pictures is a way to inhabit the bodies of characters as well as their minds.

—John Sayles, *Thinking in Pictures*

THE DAY BEFORE THE FUTURE BEGINS

Sometimes you get an even break. Usually you are too busy with
something else to notice it, entirely too busy to untangle the webs of
significance you've spun yourself into to respond to it with anything
other than a series of already impolite utterances that with increasing
urgency become densely populated with explicatives.

It was eight A.M. when I answered the phone. I was at home, webbed in
at the computer, writing a last-minute critical response to four convention
papers about organizational cultures, a response I should have written a
month before but didn't due to other webs I was then tangled in. This
life isn't easy, despite what they show it to be like on television.

"Dr. Goodall, sorry to be troubling you at home. This is Susan." Susan
is our departmental secretary and my protector from things she knows I
would rather not do, so when she is sorry to be troubling me at home it
means something has either gone terribly wrong or is about to.

"What's the problem?" Surrounding me is the rich voice of Karl Haas,
the National Public Radio classical music man, having a little fun with
the role laughter plays in sonatas, showing us what a giggle sounds like
when it is derived from a joke played in a musical scale.

"Bonny just called, and ———— [a high-ranking university official] is

53

anxious to get in touch with you." Bonny is that high-ranking university official's secretary. Now I know something has gone terribly wrong or is about to.

"Why? Has my tenure been revoked?" Behind me is a musical giggle, a few little piano notes having fun with the fingers.

Susan laughs. "No, nothing like that. A high-ranking university official has had a last-minute cancellation for this weekend's trip to Space Camp and since you're the first alternate he wants to know if you can join the group."

There is mischief afoot here. "I didn't know I was an alternate. Hell, I didn't even know there was a trip to Space Camp!"

"Well, you are. And there is. And that's that." Susan giggles. Karl Haas laughs. "What should I tell him for you?"

This is the part of the conversation that is a series of impolite utterances that with increasing urgency become densely populated with explicatives.

"Thank you, Dr. Goodall. I'll call right away and tell Bonny you are sorry you can't attend."

Karl Haas is laughing as I retreat back into my webs.

I suffer guilt despite the fact that I am not Catholic.

Back at my computer I am filled with it. Deep wells of it gush from the core of my being, flood into my vital organs, wash over all my sensitivities, and drench my mind with a cosmic blankness.

I feel low. Then I am low and in a bad place. After that I am low and in a bad place where no matter how I try to write this convention paper it comes out flat. Then I am even lower. So low I am flat.

Not even my loyal retrievers want to share my space. Together they leave the room with only flat me in it.

Repentance is possible.

This is not a bad break I've been given, but an even one.

This is an opportunity. Besides, I am flat if I stay here.

So I fly into the city on the wings of my Thunderbird, reverse my previous decision, make a claim in the presence of Bonny about really wanting to go, and back it up with evidence of my interest in writing about the experience.

Susan finds my plea amusing. Behind me at the office while I am on the phone she giggles, then breaks out into an outright belly laugh.

So does my wife when I ask her permission to go off to camp, Space Camp, for the weekend.

DAY ONE

Forty of us assemble at 7:15 at the Training Center on 1 Tranquility Drive, a place known as the Earth's Largest Space and Rocket Museum. The sign on the door reads, "Through these doors pass the future leaders, scientists, and astronauts of the United States of America."

This is an earthly building made to imitate our collective vision of the future, a future of odd, functional angles and occasional geodesic domes, a place to represent the interface between a warm world of gravity and oxygen and a cool technology text. From behind this structure rise the fuel tanks and nose cones of recent American history, from the Mercury smallships to the Apollo tallships, a circular flash of celebrations, brilliant white memories upon which our flag and the initials of our nation are all that is left to remind us of our earthly parameters.

There is, oddly, an expansive feeling of nostalgia we feel for those first space pioneers, the men and later the women who, like Columbus, gambled with their lives for the rewards of that which they could not even imagine. But after the nostalgia retreats, another feeling assembles itself around these rockets and cones. This is a feeling of fear and history, a feeling that reminds us that rocketry was first used for the singular purpose of death and enslavement by a German regime that goose-stepped and screamed, "V-2! V-2!! V-2!!!"

We are brought inside by a complement of blue-flight-suited youths, our trainers and guides for this three-day mission.

I am struck by their Republican good looks and singular sense of purpose. We are marched through a line to collect our information packets, badges, the black-and-gold SPACE ACADEMY caps that we are instructed to wear. When we get to the desk with the stack of blue flight suits we find that they can be bought for $74.95 (no charge cards, please!). We also find that the members of this group who are not from the university, people I will later learn who have paid the full $450 tuition and who have traveled here from all over America, England, and Canada to share this experience, are given their suits. They immediately zipper themselves into them with smiles of anticipation.

We are then grouped into three teams: *Enterprise, Discovery,* and *Pathfinder.* I am put on the *Enterprise,* and the first thought I have is "Beam me up, Scotty!" Even then, at the beginning of this weekend, I do not think this is an accident.

We are photographed as a group, all wearing our caps, surrounded by the blue-flight-suited youths who will supervise our acquisition of information and skills. And then we are told to march out to the buses, the blue-and-white NASA tour buses that wear the ALL-AMERICAN labels.

Tommy Ellison is our guide. He is a polite, well-dressed, enthusiastic, conservative man in early middle age with thinning brown hair and matching glasses, just old enough to joke about encountering the early space program in his "Weekly Reader" during the '50s, a line that brings a laugh from those of us who were also in grade school at the time.

For those of us who have lived in Huntsville, the Marshall Space Flight Center is no big deal. For anyone else it is roughly equivalent to spending the next two hours being able to watch, but not touch, your favorite technological fantasy. We are brought in through the security gates and parked next to buildings in which the past, present, and future of space travel was, is, and will be made possible (never mind about a Houston or a Kennedy!). Here is where some of the astronauts trained for space flight and where serious scientific work on all of the missions is conducted.

The tourists among us locals are uniformily impressed. We are shown the space shuttle mock-up and encouraged to look around in it, to move into the living and command quarters and touch the fabrics and plastics. Ditto for the space station mock-up, ditto again for the huge water tank with the space station simulation inside where zero-gravity conditions are achieved by attaching weights to the astronauts. And so forth.

These buildings are stark places, havens for technological and scientific advancements. Nothing is playful, no entertaining symbols, and few, if any, smiles. Around us work is going on, and we are introduced, as if by accident, to the scientist who created the variable-polarity arc welder, told that he won "Inventor of the Year" for it. He offers to demonstrate and an enthusiastic crowd circles around him. His name is Bayless, and he is a short handsome man, the kind of red-haired person whom you sort of instantly like. He speaks with a Southern accent with an even Baptist reverence for his subject, seems a bit too humble to be doing this on a regular basis. He hands a mask to a person in the front and asks them to step around the shield to watch the welder in action.

This is no display, incidentally, this is a real-life, real-work, real-time project. The arc welder flashes. We are casually told the light will blind us if we look directly into it, so we don't. The light spill during the weld surrounds us nevertheless, a brighter light than anything anyone has ever lived in before. The visitors are amazed. Bayless smiles. He shakes a few hands. Tommy Ellison leads us away.

Over my shoulder I notice Bayless walk back toward the computer room. These PR stunts have probably interrupted him, brought him out like a trained seal to perform a rote feat for a crowd. Is this what it means to be "Inventor of the Year?" On the way out I notice the inner offices, look for clues in signs. The only sign I see is a familiar poster with a monkey and a banana: "Just Hang in There Till Friday!"

All this in a building named "Productivity Enhancement."

Back on the bus I am seated next to James McPike, a scholar from the history department.

James is a thin, quiet man about my age with an easy smile who has probably been railroaded into this weekend at camp because this is his tenure year. Last week he asked if I would serve as the outside person on his tenure committee; that was perhaps the first time I had more than a single-sentence conversation with him. His area is Eisenhower. I ask about his new book on Eisenhower and how he got interested in him.

"I was working on something else for a dissertation when my advisor suggested I look into Eisenhower. The university had a collection, it was close by, so . . ." James has just told me one of the archetypal stories of how scholars get their starts. Within the culture of academe most of us are drawn broadly into a field that encourages us to become more narrow if we plan to pursue careers. We stumble onto projects with advisors, work in areas of research that are fundable at the moment. I mention this because it seems to be no different for those persons I have known who are involved in the space program. Among humans, accidents happen and coincidences occur; only later do we try to attribute motive and purpose.

For technology and science the opposite is true. The opposite, in fact, is truth.

Back at the Space and Rocket Center we are given our shuttle orientation. "Call me Sledge," our instructor says, "and listen up."

Sledge looks exactly like you think someone young with that name and obvious sense of macho should look. He carries himself proudly, struts across his stage explaining the process we will experience during the next three days. Call him Maverick, I am thinking, put him in a movie about fast planes and girlfriends.

He lectures and (I mentally respond):

"The commander and pilot go in first about one and one-half hours prior to lift-off." (Yes, but what do they think about? How do they feel?)

He asks us what the water is for that we see pouring down the sides of the shuttle (by the way, he struts, the shuttle is what we call the whole thing, the commander and pilot and crew ride in the *orbiter*) prior to lift-off. Cooling, we respond.

"Wrong! It is used to absorb sound and to dampen vibration caused by the firing of the thrusters. We use about 300,000 gallons in thirty seconds.

"At T minus fifteen seconds the orbital computers take over. And we begin shooting sparks across the bottoms of the engines to prevent a hydrogen explosion on the launch pad." (*Now* how do the astronauts feel, knowing this?)

"The main engines are fired before the solid rocket boosters (SRBs) because we can't shut off the SRBs once they are fired." (And *now* . . . ?)

"It takes a full five seconds to build up enough thrust for lift-off. During this time the white clouds that explode out from beneath the shuttle engines are caused by the steam from the rapidly evaporating water. About that time you see the TWANG effect—when the nose of the shuttle seems to pull back like a rubber band prior to lift-off." (My God! What do the riders think about *that*?)

"The shuttle is held in place by eight huge bolts [he rolls one over for us to look at, and we see a bolt about as long as a full-grown golden retriever and about as thick as good chunk of firewood] that contain explosive charges to break them from the stud acceleration stand. It is definitely Criticality 1 if we don't blow off the bolts prior to lift-off." (He doesn't explain what would happen, and I'm not sure I really want to know.)

"When the shuttle clears the tower the responsibility for the flight shifts from Kennedy to Johnson." (This is something I've always wondered about. Why bother? Is it because of politics or is there a reason for this shift?)

"First thing that the astronauts experience is the roll maneuver, where they turn the ship into a heads-down position. Then they throttle down to reduce aerodynamic loading on the launch vehicle. Then staging begins.

"About two minutes into flight the psi on the SRBs is less than 50 percent—this means that there is less than half a tank of fuel in them.

At this point they become a liability to the shuttle. Four motors are fired on the SRBs to push them away from the orbiter; each of the motors burns for six-tenths of a second.

"Then the OMES (orbital maneuvering engine system) is activated, producing 6,000 foot-pounds of thrust to maneuver the orbiter into orbit. This is called OMES-1 burn.

"Once in orbit we open the cargo doors to expose the heat radiators. These dispel heat from the orbiter and if they can't be opened we are in big trouble." (He doesn't go into details)

"Once that maneuver is completed, the flight begins. If you go to the space station the EVAs (extra-vehicular activities) begin, if you work in the Spacelab the experiments begin."

Here is the part where, I imagine, we are drifting, floating, flying. And working. Here, right here.

What is it like? What do the people aboard think about?

No words from Sledge on this one.

"When you come home you need to close the cargo doors, burn the OMES engines to slow down the orbiter, which actually causes you to speed up while you descend because the farther away you are from the earth the longer it takes to make an orbit so when you slow down and decrease your orbit you actually are going faster.

"Then we slam into the atmosphere at about Mach 25. The orbiter builds up heat rapidly due to friction. When we hit the ion layer all radio communications are disrupted. During this time the heat shields protect the orbiter." (Yes, if they are still in place!)

"Upon entry you regain radio communications with Houston and perform the S-turns that allow you to manage the energy of the craft and to slow down for your approach to the runway. You make your approach at twenty-two degrees glidescope, moving at 190 knots, and require about fifteen thousand feet of runway.

"That's it, folks!" Sledge grins. "You're back home." (Yes, if you are very lucky.)

We are free for lunch. Before I go to the cafeteria I move into the barracks.

I have been assigned to the Red Room, which is actually the color of the door to the room, not the room itself. Once inside I find rows of double-decker bunks and green, gym-style lockers. The beds aren't made, there are no towels, and this is not exactly what I had in mind. I'm more of a Marriott man, myself. I stash my bags in a convenient locker and look around for a bathroom.

The sign on the door says "Waste Management: Men."

I should have known.

After lunch we are taken back to the Bubble, divided into nine groups, and told to go to our training stations.

I am scheduled for mission practice, which is the training for my first assignment as weather and traffic officer–Houston. Our instructor is Vicki, an engineering student at the University who at eighteen is definitely all business about this. We are told that if we screw up, the shuttle will abort or crash.

We are strongly encouraged not to screw up.

My seat is behind a simulator that includes a full complement of toggle switches and lights, a computer screen with weather data, and a headphone set. There are nine of us in here behind similar simulators, each with a specific job to simulate, all of us connected to each other and to the shuttle via headsets, facing big simulation screens with changing slides and moving pictures. Just like in the movies!

In front of each of us is a script book divided into sections. On the inside jacket are my "Rules" and "Instructions" manuals, which I am encouraged to stay up tonight memorizing. How tough can that be? There are only three rules and three short pages of instructions; I think I'll go to bed tonight instead.

The script is broken down by minutes and seconds that begin at "T minus nine minutes and holding" and take us moment by moment, line by line, through a variety of simulated possibilities. We are told that this practice time will be devoted to learning what can go wrong, in the event that when the "real thing" happens we will know what to do.

Basically there are three major events that can go wrong when you fly the shuttle. The first occurs at T minus six seconds and is called an RSLS abort (redundant shuttle launch systems), and if you don't deal with it *immediately* the shuttle can't be launched without serious problems. This time I ask what that means. "Specifically," Vicki says, evenly, "this means exploding on the launch pad."

Glad I asked.

The second major problem occurs once the shuttle has been launched successfully and is in flight. This problem is caused by a failure in the

OMES system and is called "abort to orbit." The flight can continue, but no one ever explained to me how the astronauts can return home without OMES support. OMES support, incidentally, includes forty-four small engines that are used to maneuver the vehicle and without which vehicle maneuvering is impossible. So I guess without OMES support, you are lost in the impossible.

The third major problem occurs when the orbiter returns from its mission. If the OMES burn is successful there is still the problem of weather. What if the primary landing site is under a severe thunderstorm watch? Certainly wouldn't want to land there. So the weather and traffic officer (that's me!) has to make a recommendation to the mission director about alternatives, such as Kennedy or White Sands.

In addition to these three major sources of abort, there are a host of built-in nonterminal problems for the crew of the orbiter, the space station EVA crew, and the Houston ground-control team to deal with. We are told that on a previous flight the pilot of the orbiter locked his landing brakes prior to lowering his landing gear, thus causing the 165,000 pound bird to crash on the runway, slide along its heat shields, and essentially ruin everyone's whole day.

I look over to my left at Grant Thomas, the former chair of the math department and now the SSO officer, and grin. He grins back and shakes his head. To my right sits Lou Jarold, an engineering professor currently serving as public affairs officer for this flight; he is trying to memorize his part. Vicki comes over the phones and, in a stern voice, reminds us that this is not a game, but a simulation. Everyone has to work together or she will be very upset.

Very upset.

Nobody laughs after that.

The remainder of the first afternoon is spent learning the equipment of space flight.

My team experiences (near) weightlessness in the one-sixth-gravity chair and discovers that the ideal spacewalker weighs 150 pounds. Those of us who arrived here larger than that have a much easier time with the machine, but are disappointed to find that we are too large for the real fun of the simulator.

The maneuvering pod simulator is an egg-shaped plastic bubble that rises up at about two Gs of force through a glass tube and then is dropped back down at full force of gravity. This one looks like a lot of fun. However, we are told in strategically ambiguous terms that anyone over six feet tall cannot be allowed in it.

Phillip, a Welsh theoretical materials scientist who has just come over to the university after spending a year as a visiting scientist at NASA, and I are the only two campers in our flight over six feet tall. Oh well. Not only am I too heavy for outer space, I am now also too tall.

Our third task is accomplished despite height or weight disadvantages.

It is called the multi-axis chair. It is used to simulate total disorientation of your equilibrium. Watching it operate it appears, however, to serve a different purpose, specifically to see whether or not you vomit when spun around and about at varying speeds and at differing angles while your body is strapped down to a seat with your hands strapped up to steel bars. Phillip and I, figuring we'd already missed out on some of the nuances of the experience of space, volunteer for this one.

Seated in the chair you feel strangely like a trapped monkey. You know something is going to happen, that it probably won't be pleasant, but there is nothing you can do about it. Language won't help.

After I am "secured," the technician begins the exercise. What happens is difficult to describe linearly. The appropriate analogy might be that this is what the chaos of multiple causality feels like when it is done to your person. You are totally out of control, off the earth, and there is nothing to do except go with it. Psychologically it is similar to dropping acid when the first rush comes and you realize fully the implications of what you've done. Focusing on that thought I begin giggling, and by the time the "ride" is over I am laughing hysterically.

Phillip enjoys it so much he goes twice.

Only one person actually throws up.

After that experience we are marched back up to the training center for the GMMU (ground manned maneuvering unit) exercise.

In space this is called an MMU because it is no longer on the ground, and it is used to fly around the spaceship or make repairs. However, at Space Camp it is little more than a chair attached to an electronic motor that is in turn mounted to four feet that bear remarkable resemblance to floor polishers. If this is how they actually train astronauts, they could just as easily use it to train househusbands. No fun. No fun at all.

Back at the Bubble we are run through a one-hour practice session, complete with two aborts, for our first mission.

Oddly enough, there is a feeling of anticipation combined with a distinct desire to do well among the participants. No one wants to screw up! This is serious business!

We screw up anyway.

During the countdown an RSLS abort is ordered but those of us in mission control–Houston don't notice that the shuttle is still on the launchpad until we are about two minutes into the flight. Vicki is clearly disappointed, and frankly, so are we. We resolve to do better next time.

The experience is memorable because time goes quickly and there is much to do. People suddenly ask you for data that you have to find. Switches must be thrown in the proper sequence. If a light doesn't come on, it must be reported to the right person *immediately*. There are a lot of surprises that you wouldn't expect from reading the script. Add to this the human potential for error, which is vast, and the fact that there are three teams of adults connected only by audio and video equipment, all of whom have jobs that must be done with the cooperation of each other.

Time continues even when you don't.

After we manage to land successfully we are all suddenly up from our chairs cheering, hats are tossed, a cigar is lit. Mission accomplished! And then we realize what has happened to us. Here we are, a bunch of college professors, all adults and most of us old enough to be our simulation director's parent, and we have been so drawn into the event that the thin line that always exists between fantasy and reality has been lost, or perhaps so blurred as to become indistinguishable.

Soaked with real sweat we leave the simulation room. Still feeling the exhilaration of doing what we have only seen done on television, not wanting to admit that what we were doing was entering the video world ourselves, pushing back this particular envelope to the extent that we have entered the mysteries of the other side, we go. Living in video.

At dinner there is a sense of spirit that most of us who have worked with each other for years have never really known. There is also some silliness in all this. We know that.

Don't we?

We watch as a couple of silvery jets scream across the dusky sky.

This first night under the twinkling pleasures of a fine autumn starlight, we are moved into the Spacedome to watch the OmniMax film *Hail, Columbia!*

Many of us have seen it before. But as in any good film or piece of propaganda, each time we see it we see more in it. Partly this is because the Spacedome theater consists of fairly comfortable reclining seats and a giant screen that covers 180 surround degrees to delight the eyes. Because of the angle of the seating, the eyes are always directed upward.

For a moment prior to the beginning of the film I think of *The Rise and Fall of the Third Reich.* Particularly I think of the footage of the Hitler Youth, all decked out in their uniforms, filled with authority and a collective sense of purpose. I think also of the first uses of film for propaganda purposes. There is nothing intentional in these musings, but I do notice that they have arisen within me as a response to the situation I am experiencing.

Claude Lévi-Straus teaches us to look at nature and culture as opposites and to find in cultural artifacts, such as films, traces of these binary footprints in the images and icons they reveal. My friend David Whillock taught me how to use this technique and it has changed forever the way I watch films.

So this night, in the Spacedome, this is what I see:

From the opening shot of the shuttle on the launch pad we are confronted with binary opposites. Beneath the shuttle (up and down placement is important here) lies the earth, a swampy marshland that suggests all that is primitive and natural. About halfway through the film this image is repeated; this time the lens focuses on the humorous plight of a frightened, lost armadillo in the marshland, and above him a solitary hawk squawks at the orbiter.

There is a wind in these sequences that moves the grasses, makes subtle waves on the water, blows through the astronauts' hair. In this sequence of frames there is a sense of constraint that is difficult to define. A cramped and claustrophobic feeling emerges from the screen, due perhaps to the loudness and crowding of persons and things into this down environment where the only way out is up on the shuttle to some infinite depth of freedom, an escape from inner to outer space.

Against these symbolic displays of the effects of gravity we are given the contrast of a vast, silent, and weightless space. Up there beyond the junk and the atmosphere is the 17,500 miles-per-hour floating orbit of the truly free. This feeling is, of course, an illusion. How can you be free when you are trapped inside of something moving that fast?

Constantly in these shots we are reminded of earth. She is a blue and white Easter egg that from afar appears to be a perfect and tranquil paradise, a home made for the chosen people by a truly omnipotent, and artistically talented, God.

The closer we get, the further we slip away from this mystical vision. As we travel back into the atmosphere and gravity of this planet we begin to make out the lights of cities, the roadways that connect places, and the rank pollution of humankind. Perhaps this is part of the anxiety of reentry, an anxiety caused not merely by the digital demands of measurable conditions, but also by the emotions we can only associate with earth, emotions that allow us to recognize beauty without that being enough, to be driven beyond understanding and appreciation for the blue planet to some damned need to dominate and control it. And to pronounce what we have done *progress*.

The hero of this film is John Young, macho veteran astronaut, moonwalker, press conference ace. His counterpart in this dialect of intricate opposites is John Crippen, the unveteraned, quieter participant in this dramatic display. Young has all the right lines and Crippen has all the right responses to those lines, and the only thing they appear to share beyond the orbiter is their first name.

The hero and his novice are shown preparing for the flight, and with them we rise upward into the peace of a cloudless day in a cockpit made for two. We soar silently at speed and watch the wonder of jets at play in the baby blue pastures of the wild blue yonder.

Back on the ground they are hounded by the press, who want to know what will happen if the heat-shield tiles peel off the bottom of the orbiter upon reentry. Crippen is a silent shadow played against the brutal, macho honesty of Young, who tells us that he doesn't believe there is going to be a problem, but if there is the orbiter will burn up, and by implication both of these heroes will die on fire in the air in front of us.

This is not, of course, what happens. However, for those of us who watched the explosion of the later *Challenger* shuttle flight L-51, it is a haunting forecast of that trespass. For now, though, we are taken back to the lauchpad at Kennedy, shown the poor, dumb, scared armadillo, shown the fearless hawk in flight. Against this natural backdrop rises the white, virgin shuttle, a beautiful thing, a mysterious wonder of the world, an achievement of an advanced technological society.

We are shown a waiting, excited audience of boosters, against which the booster rockets rise on a maximum screen. Quickly the astronauts don their suits and move into the orbiter, quickly we are taken back to the crowd, to the looks of anxious anticipation on faces below which are worn various symbols of patriotism. The countdown begins.

There is a problem. It is a problem with two of the onboard computers, something (we are reassured by the voice-over) that has never occurred before. The decision is made to cancel the flight.

The crowd is deeply disappointed. There are tears. The astronauts emerge with a momentary, barely concealed display of anger and frustration, which is articulated by the sympathetic voice of the narrator.

I wonder about this sequence in the movie, about the strategy of it. We all know that in any heroic film, any piece of propaganda, there must be a struggle against which the hero is pitted. By overcoming what seems to be frighteningly bad odds, the hero transcends the ordinary human condition and becomes heroic. Perhaps that is all there is to this strategy in the film. After all, this sequence did, in fact, occur.

But there also seems to be another factor at work here. It is the Burkean sense of progressive form in which a desire is created early on that is—through resolution of some essential conflict—finally, and triumphantly, satisfied. "Form *is* the appeal," he reminds us, and it functions as "the creation of an appetite."

If this logic is true, the audience for this film should identify with the audience for the shuttle launch—not with the astronauts, at least not yet. What we are asked to do in the language of this film is to relive an experience we have already lived through in the past, but this time to enter it at a more intimate distance and to share it with strangers. Our struggle is perhaps to find a cause to release a common emotion, an emotion of satisfaction, that will move this shared experience from the private to the public sphere. And so we move into the video world, join symbolically with the crowd, and together push toward this desperately needed emotional release, crowding out the reasonable message of the subtext (*this is dangerous* and *computers/technology have failed*) in favor of the emotional demands of the situation. What we need here, put simply, is a climax.

The scene is set once again. This time there are fewer observers, no armadillo, no hawk. Is our previous disappointment with the failure to launch going to be repeated? Or are we to move along in this filmic progression to climax, get on with the business of success in outer space?

Quickly we get to the countdown and those powerful rockets fire, sending out and over us a stunning display of smoke, steam, power, and color as the shuttle lifts off and rises into glory. The crowd cheers as the flight continues, driven to a frenzy by its raw, thundering cadence, amazed by its sheer force, a force that will lift us beyond the rocket fiction of gravity's rainbow and into a totally new Hollywood vision of life in space.

The flight is smooth, comforting, and quiet. Now come the magnificent views of earth from above, from the perspective of God, and the blue planet where once blossomed a peaceful and perfect paradise seems astonishingly beautiful. Suspended in awe and in thought and in the warm, emotional afterglow of the powerful lift-off's surging climax, we are taken around the world in seconds, and around the world again. And again.

But our formal progression is not yet complete.

There is the anticipation of reentry, that most dangerous phase of the mission that requires the fiery burst back into earth's atmosphere and then, if all goes well, the first landing of the earth's only true spaceship. Again the tension mounts, and the screen is alive with it. We are brought into Houston's mission control where radio contact has been lost and anxiety is the only resident emotion. Fat men, skinny men, men in white shirts and men in loosened black ties are teetering on the edge of precisely what we feel ourselves, even though we already know the outcome.

Suddenly the voice of Young crackles through the electricity and there is renewed hope and work to be done. The wide-angle camera moves out to the landing site, back to the crowd, captures again the evident emotions, the surround of an anticipatory hero's welcome, against which the cosmic blankness of the desert forms a subtle, natural contrast. In swoops the beautiful orbiter, in it swoops and down it glides, perfectly back to earth and smoothly down the runway.

We are sated.

The heroes emerge and are happy!

We have done as an audience what no audience has ever done before!

For the next few minutes we are allowed to relive the original climax as we are given three different angles of the lift-off, three different interpretations of the same event, three sources of a curious mix of arousal and satisfaction, the perfecting of a form of human experience.

When the lights go up we are applauding and do not immediately wish to leave the place where it happened. But as we look quickly back and forth at each other there seems to be nothing else left to do.

If I were a smoker, this would be the time to light a cigarette. To pronounce it good.

A small group of us decide to play hooky for the rest of the evening, down a few drinks at the neighboring bar.

It is a clear night, just on the verge of the harvest moon, the sort of cool autumn evening that inspires discourse about the meanings of things and the motives of people. The wind is light, the stars friendly.

A few of us walk over to the bar exchanging impressions about our Space Camp experience. I am with Eli, a member of the English department and is also one of the most intelligent and sensitive beings on this planet, according to me. He tells us that today he has learned how much he appreciates gravity.

"Gravity?" This probably from me, although my recollection of who said what in this lightning exchange is unclear.

"Yes. Gravity gives me everything I value. Take it away and there is no wind, no touch, no movement, nothing."

"So you didn't enjoy the weightlessness?"

"It lacks intimacy. It's boring. Everything is equal, digital, on or off. It's like math." He grins.

In the Marriott's bar, which is just a bar with the usual ferns and soft colors, we are joined by Phillip and an Arab scientist whose name was never pronounced clearly enough for me to understand.

I ask Phillip how he got involved in space science.

"I was reared in South Wales, by the sea. I collected rocks as a child."

"But why become a scientist? Why not just go on collecting rocks?"

He smiles easily. "Watching 'Dr. Who' on the tele."

Everyone stares.

"Really. All my friends watched it, organized our schedules around it. It's a gas."

"Do you remember a show called 'Bill and Ben, the Flowerpot Men?' "

"Yes! That too! How did you know about that?"

I tell him it was a formative part of my youth. When I lived in England it was my favorite show. Basically it is the adventures of two vaguely intelligent, talking flowers that grow in a windowsill and play jokes on their gardener. "It was the first head show," I finish.

"So then what?" I am digging into Phillip's motives.

"So then I went to university, got a degree in geology. Toward the end I realized there wasn't much need for another geologist so I applied to graduate school over here. Got really interested in crystals."

"Another degree in geology?"

"No, oceanography." He looks playful about this. "Don't ask why."

I don't.

"I worked for a while in Florida and hated it. There wasn't much money, I had to get a second job in the summer. So I quit. Called a friend and asked if he knew anything going on that might be interesting and he told me he had just talked to a fellow at Carnegie who needed a postdoctoral assistant, so I went up there for three years.

"One day I was watching a PBS show about crystal growth in zero gravity and got really excited. I didn't know NASA was involved in basic science, just never thought about it. I told my advisor about it and he asked me if I would be interested in working for NASA. I said sure, and he made some calls, and I came down here as a visiting scientist."

"What do you like about crystals?"

"They are very beautiful, neat rocks."

We are joined by some more Space Campers, including a college dean. He looks tired, says he's tired, orders a drink. Emphatically orders a drink. He's just come back from his mission on the simulator and everyone wants to know how it went.

"Crashed and burned," he says, sipping his drink. "Somebody forgot to lower the landing wheels so we skidded across the runway and destroyed the orbiter."

We laugh, for some reason.

"Our instructor said we would have to glue all the tiles back on tomorrow morning."

This is a joke. "What was your job?"

"I was a monkey in the payload bay, running experiments." He sips thoughtfully. "This whole thing has confirmed my deepest fears about NASA. There is no good reason to send human beings into outer space. There is nothing that can't be done as well by robots or monkeys."

Back at the barracks I open the red door and walk into a room of middle-aged men in boxer shorts struggling to fit themselves into bunks designed for children. One of them is already producing a loud and mournful snore whose echo is chased by small pitiful whine.

Somebody farts and apologizes.

Someone bangs what I take to be a kneecap on a metal railing trying to reach a top bunk, issues an impertinent order to one Jesus Christ.

I am inebriated and discover I have no bedsheets.

Through these doors pass the future American
leaders, scientists, and astronauts . . .

You bet.

DAY TWO

Saturday morning we are wakened by light, told to rise and shine. It is 6:15. We are supposed to wash and dress and hustle up to the mess hall for breakfast. We do.

For those campers who exercised free will the night before and slunk to the comfort of their own beds and homes in Huntsville, this early hour seems comparatively beautiful and true. For the rest of us, those who labored through the night, locked alongside tortured snorers and worse, there is a certain testiness.

We share a breakfast in small groups about which hover a bored, anxious, collective silence.

For the first hours of instruction we are marched back into the bubble and introduced to our second mission assignments. I am to be a scientist, unlikely even under the best of simulated conditions, and I must carry out an elaborate background radio noise experiment whose written in-structions are far more difficult than the actual task, which is to flip toggle switches in a particular sequence. I must also lift weights and write down which weight seems heavier. If there is time left, I must ride an exercise bicycle and record my pulse rates.

The dean was right. Monkey business, if you ask me.

Having been denied my second cup of caffeine and ordered about like an animal somewhat further down on the food chain than I had previously assumed myself to be, I confront the simulation director and demand to know the purpose of these experiments.

He looks at me evenly. "You don't need to know," he says, "and this is a need-to-know operation."

I was a debater in college and accustomed by the conditions of my later employment as an academic administrator to deal directly with the difficult. "Don't you think it would be helpful for the trainees to know what mysteries their work will solve?"

"No," he replies. "What you need to understand is that you have a job to do. It is one job. Back at Johnson there are scientists whose job it will be to process what you do up here. They also have one job. What makes the whole thing work is that everyone does his or her job and doesn't try to understand any other jobs."

"What happens if something goes wrong? Don't you think it would help if everyone was trained to carry out a variety of jobs?"

"No," he replies. "That doesn't make any sense." And then he walks away.

After I learn that I don't make any sense I am marched back up to the Rocket Center for a lecture by a famous rocket scientist, one of the original Peenemunde group who came over after the double digit war to help make America great.

He appears before the group sporting a sharp suit and crisply pressed blue shirt and fashionable tie. He takes his place before the models of rocket engines he helped create and begins.

"Pipple vant to know vat iz her *rocket!*" From his shirt pocket he produces a small red balloon and after some difficulty blows up it up, releases it before our very eyes. "Dis iz her *rocket!*"

It is a delightful little display, perfectly adequate for children and academics.

As he continues to speak about his early days with the mythic Von Braun team I am struck by the forcefulness of his voice, its commanding, superior directness, a voice that has never questioned itself or the source of its native authority. I am also struck by the fact that his microphone isn't operating properly, and each heavily accented, forceful sentence is shot alternately through the left and right speakers in this arena.

During the next few minutes the famous rocket scientist gives a masterful lecture on the principles of rocketry, including some amusing anecdotes about the problems of applying those principles to various projects. At one point he recounts a memory of the German V-2 with an almost wistful sense of irony, refers to the potatoes grown in Poland that were distilled into rocket fuel because there was no gasoline allotment from Hitler, and uses the term "Greater Germany." Here is a man who has no regrets, I am thinking, who gives the impression that if only there had been a little more gasoline . . .

I begin to narrow my focus of vision to his tiepin. It is a small, gold one in the shape of something I can't quite make out. As he continues his historical lesson and moves from the glory days of Greater Germany to the postwar superpower United States, from the shattered factories of Peenemunde to the sleepy cotton fields of was-then Huntsville, he steps toward me. I keep my eyes on his tiepin, and then it happens. I see it for precisely what it is.

It is the golden head of the Trojan horse.

An epiphany commences. This is too much symbolism for me. I calm myself with the understanding that this assessment lives only in my own interior conversations, and I can break from it if I want to.

But I choose not to.

The famous rocket scientist thunders on in a rich, vibrant rhetorical style that punctuates the necessity of action, demands from its hearers absolute obedience, does not believe it can be wrong. This voice could, I think, inspire a crowd of youngsters to do seemingly impossible things, unnatural things, like—pardon me for this one—invade Poland for the purpose of acquiring its potatoes.

Following his talk we are herded into the famous Rocket Park behind the Earth's Largest Space Museum, a stunning display of our rocket prowess. Here are the dream erections of an advanced technological society, the ultimate expression of a decidedly masculine science. Here are the solid white rockets of the whole earth's most powerful turbocharged engines atop which rode the experimental seamen in a tiny, tiny capsule resembling a perfect circumcision.

It is here that the famous rocket scientist waxes technical. We are told that stage one of the Saturn V rocket creates the power of eighty-five Hoover dams, 7.5 million pounds of thrust at lift-off, and makes a stereo surround equal to 200 million watts. It was the biggest bang in the universe since that old original one, if you don't count the ineffable atomic flashes over Hiroshima and Nagasaki.

A couple of the older guys in the crowd are clearly uncomfortable about this. Old enough to have fought against the famous rocket scientist's boss, they find themselves forty years later dressed up in flight suits politely listening to an apparently unreformed ex-Nazi. For them, there must be a certain sense of déjà vu.

In my head appears an image of my dead father. He was a man who, in 1944, at the age of twenty-two, was shot down over Germany and turned into a prisoner of war. He was liberated there with two paralyzed legs that he suffered through a peacetime life of government service that claimed him too young. Thinking of him under the famous rocket scientist's thunder, I get that feeling too. I don't know what it is but something washes over me with tiny, prickly particles made from a part of the past I didn't live through but now feel I have touched.

I make my way to the back of the crowd with the old guys. Together, like the green dinosaurs in a Gary Larson cartoon, we grin at the Artist with the corrupt sweetness of certain extinction.

After lunch we are taken in mass into a gaudy auditorium to hear a chief project scientist discuss the Hubble Space Telescope.

His talk is full of visual aids, which is good, because otherwise I would declare this period naptime. I notice that some of my fellow campers have done so. How someone can take a subject as potentially exciting and awe-inspiring as this marvelous telescope and render it uncommonly boring is beyond me; but he does it.

Mostly he does it with numbers. Sentence after sentence was monotonously delivered in which action verbs are replaced with states-of-being statistics, and whole opportunities for nominative absolutes are given up in favor of bland technical descriptions. If this is what engineers like, I'm glad I didn't turn out to be one.

We are told that this machine can deliver .007 (he pauses; get the joke?) arc seconds of stability at two hundred miles, which is like being able to see a dime on a sidewalk in New York City with a laser beam mounted in Washington, D.C.

Now does that sort of talk really turn you on?

Great technical achievement, but why bother? What's the mystery here?

At one point in the talk this chief Do-Da mentions the fact that the Hubble will allow us to see the beginning of the universe—back there about 14 billion years or so. He says it precisely, with no attendant emotion. He says it just like that, and then moves on.

This is the world where everything is equal, Eli had told me, like math.

But what is the subtext here?

The talk turns to the problem of storage for his completed marvelous thing, which, as the accompanying visual aid shows us, makes ordinary men wear plastic and masks as they gather in a glass cathedral known as a "clean room" to watch for signs of "contamination." What is particularly striking about this visual is the image of the telescope itself, a marvelous cylinder against which, about three-quarters of the way up, is a wrapping made into a perfect and big burgundy cross.

No explanation is given for that. I guess this is the sort of science where symbols have no meanings.

Except, of course, for the continuous and repetitive message that this technological wonder comes with a pricetag of $1.5 billion. I make a note that reads: Numbers are symbols of a different sort because their apparent neatness and precision blurs the fact that what they do to us is far more important than what they are.

Our second movie is *The Dream Is Alive* and is played in the Spacedome. This is a newer film, cleverly done by the astronauts themselves with high-intensity visuals and Uncle Walter's voice-over.

The point of this experience is to induce the audience to believe they have moved from the role of exterior respondents to the launch and recovery of the shuttle to the role of interior participants in the flight. We are literally brought inside that fantastic orbiter, and our experience of the film is a concentrated journey around the world.

First, however, we are given a participant's view of space training. In one of our most intense moments we are released in the escape vehicle and by force of mass and gravity riveted back against our seats, sucked earthward at ever-increasing speed, and caught in a giant orange webbing.

Then we are launched into orbit. There in the alien peace that is outer space we are inside the shuttle with the crew, floating, laughing, catching bits of food in the air during dinner, sleeping with our arms out in front of us, constantly reminded by Uncle Walter how far we have advanced.

Except for the occasional shot of distant Mother Earth from one of the orbiter's windows, these scenes could pass for advertisements for new modular homes. The astronauts are attired in T-shirts and gym shorts, their muscular legs well tanned and their perfect hair combed. There is nothing to remind us that something is wrong with this picture. Women and men are working, exercising, and sleeping alone but together, just having fun up there among the stars.

In contrast to the earlier film in which a structuralist would see the nature/civilization ratios, this film presents a human/technology interface, a careful blending of women and men and machines. As we fly silently around the world at 17,500 miles per hour we are shown the boot of Italy and reminded by Uncle Walter that in that land the ultimate Renaissance man Leonardo da Vinci proclaimed that one day "Man Will Fly!"

And we are!

So full of peace and beauty and harmony between the sexes is this film about life in outer space that our occasional mental drift back into reality seems a bother. And when we land we are, perhaps like those astronauts, eager to say we are happy to be home but aware that we have left a sense of human and technological perfection behind.

When the lights come up we remember this has been a movie.

Just a movie.

I am on a bench in Rocket Park watching the tourists be entertained by the machines. I am waiting for the Lunar Odyssey experience to open, which it will not do today because of a mechanical failure.

Vico, our resident philosopher, joins me. I want to pursue with him a discussion he had this morning with our high ranking university official about how technology presents us with certain philosophical problems. I heard him argue, and I thought very effectively, about the history of science as a series of interpretive frameworks, ways of classifying the world and our place in it that were seriously altered, say, by Darwin.

Our high ranking university official, trained as a chemist and now a local champion of technology, heard all of this but did not appear to have listened to it. His interpretive framework, built it seems to me out of "can do" rather than "can doubt" material, simply could not readily accept a critique made out of words critically rendered about a world view made out of certainty in which doubt is enemy to progress.

I tell Vico this and he listens. But he does not want to talk about it, says simply, "I don't think my arguments swayed him." He seems truly saddened by this.

We talk instead about Vico's work and his travels to Ireland. There in summers he pursues his scholarship in an exotic, natural surround, writing now about the relationship between the determinate and the indeterminate, climbing rocky reefs in the mornings, drifting off to sleep late in the evening under the influence of salt air and solitude. This is where he lives his life, pursues thoughts, pursues pleasures.

Opposites exist on this earth as well.

Here we are.

Our next group experience is a lecture on the Soviet space program and I am late to it due to a duel on a video game during Lunar Odyssey downtime with James McPike, the historian.

I lost, badly.

Into the Red Room Auditorium we go, a darkened place in which a small, squat man wearing spectacles spews forth information with the style of boxing ring announcer. This is a performance! Here is the real thing!

I listen in a sort of mildly stunned way to this barrage of propaganda accompanied by spy photos. Is this the man from U.N.C.L.E. or the CIA? Every now and then he punctuates the fact of his authority by pointing out the "hours of research that have gone into this project, the countless interviews with Soviet astronauts, the trips to the USSR." No, this isn't a boxing ring announcer, but Paul Harvey on megadoses of amphetamines.

Every screen image he shows has the less-than-subtle subliminal clue "THINK SOVIET" printed in big letters across it. His intense, rapid-fire, increasingly paranoid style seems to me to undercut his credibility—who would believe Paul Harvey on speed? For this audience his assault-the-ears style is entertaining and even mildly amusing, but if this is the guy they put in front of nine-year-olds then I am truly worried.

This is Happy-the-Thrasher, a Soviet-Basher! No cooperative ventures here, not on your life! "These people," as he dirtily refers to them, "are way ahead of us, years ahead, and already have an orbiting space station and plans to go to Mars!

"They have always been this way but now we are starting to understand them! [like the retarded, perhaps?] They don't care about human life, you know, they only care about beating us out of space! Why, back when Khruschev was banging his shoe and saying he was going to bury us they were flying cosmonauts into orbit in plywood capsules, and if they wouldn't go—off to the gulag with them! We know what that's like, don't we? We wouldn't want to go, would we? I wouldn't, I can tell you, because I've talked to men and women—yes, women go to the gulag too—who have been there! Yes I have!

"One time a Soviet mission was launched without a single test of its electronic equipment and sure enough upon reentering the atmosphere the whole thing failed. Here are these heroes up there hurling toward home at many times the speed of sound and they have to sight land in the Motherland—where do they end up? In China! Yes, China, my friends, and in a snowstorm to boot! But that's not all—no, not by a long shot—these heroes crash down through the trees, land in a pile of snow and are attacked by a pack of wolves! Yes, wolves! What a welcome home!"

While he is beating back our senses with this barrage of words, the screen—"THINK SOVIET, THINK SOVIET, THINK SOVIET"—shows something that strikes me as being an important clue to how "they" are different from "us." Their spacecrafts are geodesic domes, shaped as circles, not as arrows, and look to us like alien ships, the sort of image we cannot easily identify with. In later shots—during which time this pitiful human VOICE is singing the opera of the paranoid about thesepeople THESEPEOPLE being already capable of knocking out KNOCKING OUT anything Stars Wars puts up there, anything ANYTHING, do you hear me? Am I loud enough? LOUD ENOUGH?—the image changes to a more familiar shape—due no doubt NO DOUBT, NO DOUBT to our belief in freedom and in trading scientific information FOR WHICH WE GET NOTHING IN RE-TURN, NOTHING!!—the shape of an erection pointing toward the stars.

He leaves us as breathless as he is, with a nightmarish vision of the future in which THESEPEOPLE reign over the heavens and the earth, then casually, with a shrug of the shoulders that must carry this information, he quietly mentions that our only hope is for long-term space planning and funding. FUNDING. That's it, that's our only hope, the only ticket to victory in the space race.

(So remember boys and girls, particularly when you get old enough to vote, that you get what you pay for, and if you want it you must go after it, or else you'll all end up in a gulag and there will be no United States . . .)

This is Halloween night, when the line we have only imagined blurs between the world we know and walk on and the other world which we can only fear. For a while, for a short while under the influence of scarecrow light that tonight thins forth from the harvest moon only two opposing colors to show—the orange (or is it yellow?) and the black. There is no way to know anything for sure, and no safe way out, and no safe way back from wherever you go . . .

Trick?

Or treat?

I walk into a dimly lit mission control room at T minus nine minutes and take my seat at the weather and tracking station. In front of me on the big screen is the video shuttle on the launch pad, next to it two large NASA stills. This is the real thing, my first launch.

I open my scriptbook and follow the dialogue of the control team while following my prelaunch toggle switch sequence: Cloud cover—go; visibility—go; wind velocity—go. My headphones crackle with activity; there is an urgency about doing this job, doing it well and on time.

At T minus seven and counting I switch on the three remote cameras and give a weather reading.

At T minus six and counting I lock on the first tracking-system satellite.

At T minus five and counting I lock on the second.

At T minus four and counting I lock on the third. I report to the mission director that all systems are on and functioning.

At T minus one I give a final weather reading and wish the astonauts God speed.

At T minus six seconds we pass the critical redundant systems launch sequence and the buzz of voices increases. Five, four, three, two, one, lift-off!

The mission-control team cheers as we watch the shuttle video break away from the gates and rise, powerfully, POWERFULLY, away from this earth.

Over the next few minutes I switch off the toggles I earlier switched on in reverse sequence as the flight of *Enterprise* moves according to schedule. When the script calls for it, I report mission weather and tracking status, but my attention is captured by the video of space flight—actual footage much like what we observed this afternoon at the movies—and the voices of the actors carrying out their assigned tasks.

Later the orbiter successfully docks with the space station and the EVA (extra-vehicular activity) team moves into action. The video displays them being lifted out of the bay on the long NASA arm to begin constructing a tetrahedron. On the other monitor we see the team of payload specialists move from the airlock of the shuttle into the space lab and begin, silently, to do their experiments. I am struck by the resemblance of my colleagues to the actual shuttle crews, the same businesslike faces, the same purposeful movement, a choreography of mechanical accomplishment.

The experiments and EVA activities complete, the orbiter moves away from the space station and begins its journey home. I have toggle switches to flip, weather and tracking reports to give. My screen flashes new data, and I see that the weather at our primary landing site at Edwards is turning nasty—thunderstorms, low visibility, cloud cover up to 10,000 feet.

Quickly I check the other two landing sites and find both to be acceptable. I radio my status report to the mission director and to the pilot of the orbiter, ask permission to guide them in to Kennedy instead.

Permission is granted.

A flurry of activity occurs in the room as the mission team responds to this emergency. Aboard the orbiter the crew is informed of the change, and the onboard computers are reprogrammed.

The orbiter OMES is on schedule, we lose radio contact during reentry to the fiery atmosphere, regain it a minute later and everywhere there is the necessary sigh of relief. The video screen shows the white bird homing in on schedule.

I invent a flock of seagulls on the runway and have them salute and applaud. A small joke, but the crew seems to buy into it as the pilot explains to the commander that we have to watch out for those gulls.

The orbiter lands, perfectly.

Once again, we cheer. All that is missing is the Miller Time! commercial.

Some of us regroup at the local bar, walk in decked out in our flight suits and Space Academy hats, name tags still in place.

We find ourselves surrounded by cowboys and uptown girls, cats, Ronald Reagan and Nancy, an assortment of vamps in black lace stockings and dinner jackets, a pirate, a magician, a soldier, a scientist, and a farmer.

This is Halloween, remember?

I order black Jack from a cocktail waitress young enough to be my daughter dressed in less than my wife wears when she's feeling particularly amorous. As she continues to take the orders a young woman dressed up in what she believes was "flower children" attire approaches us. Clearly the costume is not as authentic as the buzz she has on. She says to us, sincerely: "Star Warriors hurt people, so when you take this flower remember us. Please, just think about *us*." A tear from her ruby road-map eyes slides down through the peace symbol inked on her pink cheek.

She hands us, collectively, a flower.

Glides away.

Around this table is assembled a group of people who lived through the flower-child '60s that this Ms. is trying hard to simulate. Barry, our marketing expert and a real naval aviator for twenty-two years, says he feels like he ought to have a rifle to put the flower in. Tom, a research biologist, agrees.

Our waitress smiles when she asks us if we actually dressed like that, and laughs in an odd way when we admit we did. If this was a commercial we would be ordering the drink of the New Generation.

I occupy myself in a conversation with Tina, who manages a part of our research center devoted to NASA projects, talk about gaining access to decision makers for an artificial intelligence project I am working on. We have a good, professional networking interaction characteristic of what people like us are supposed to do when we meet and greet each other. I am thinking, "Is this the real simulation?"

At some point I excuse myself and head for the john. On my way there a young, inebriated couple dressed up in rented formal wear stops me. "Are you an astronaut?"

I decide to have a little fun—this is a simulation, right? "I hope to be," I say. "I'm in training now."

"Wow," they say, obviously impressed. "What do you do?"

I grin. "Classified information. But I'll tell you this much . . ." I look around the lobby for spies, lean toward them, whisper, "Mostly I play video games."

"Wowwwwww . . ."

Far out. Groovy. Where am I?

DAY THREE

It is Sunday and I am spending my free time prior to the second flight in the museum.

There is a clear and vivid message that lives out here on the display floor, a message that invites you to accept the whole picture with a kind of awe that almost makes you overlook its components. The whole picture is one of high technology revealed as a historical progression of forms that includes Mercury and Apollo capsules, lunar landers and space labs, various satellites and telescopes, tips of an iceberg. Yet couched quietly among these peaceful artifacts are instruments of destruction, from Huey helicopters fitted with rockets to Dragon antitank missiles to spy ships and atomic-powered satellites.

Buy the whole picture as a theme and you also buy into its supporting motifs. Peel back the layers of these displays and what you have is an intriguing subtext. For example, the large red Vostok Soviet space capsule is suspended directly above the decontamination chamber of the space lab display, while the rocketed Huey seemingly protects the Apollo 10 capsule. The military and atomic displays are rendered as natural counterparts to the peaceful exploration of space, and those displays in which you can directly participate—"See Your Home Region from Space!" or Arabella the Space Spider or space scales that invite you to see how much you weigh in a weightless environment—are enticements to a larger participation in something far more sinister.

Stand back and look at the people who visit here and you see a wide variety of taxpayers who have paid the price of admission to be impressed. This is a place where children often have the upper hand and are encouraged to roam freely among the videos and the displays, dreamily matching their skills against those of other children while Dad and Mom look on, perhaps also dreaming.

There is text and subtext here, and one of its masterful inventions is a language that deals predominantly with the abstract, again taking us away from the specific uses of technological achievement into a universe of discourse that has the authority to define what is most important, what is scientifically real. It is displayed here as well, and appropriately enough, as a video game in which you match words with their definitions:

alloy	crystal	eutectic
atom	crystallization	fiber optics
buoyancy	dendrite	fluid
cell	density	foam
coalesce	diffusion	glass
composite	dispersion	gradient
contact	angle dislocation	grain
containerless	dopant	gravity
processing		
contamination	electrophoresis	homogeneity
convection	enzyme	immiscible

And so forth. This is the language of power, the language of space, technology, the language of the future. Kenneth Burke tells us that such a language is counter-nature, but we tend to absorb it, redefine it, as being second nature.

I am reminded that one of the first acts of Hitler's administration was the commissioning of a new dictionary, complete, of course, with slight modifications in the definitions provided. One of them was the word "Jew," which was defined as a subhuman species. Educate a generation of children to memorize that definition and you go a long way to getting them to act toward the objects of that definition in holocaust ways.

Words that are omitted from this list include, but are not by any means limited to, human beings, peace, war, arguments, morality, ethics, communication, cooperation, reasoning, logic, intuition, decision, resistance, opposition, and power. I prefer what is left out of this picture from what is right in it.

Standing here in front of this language-of-the-future machine I gain a perspective, admittedly induced by a Burkean sense of incongruity, that "a machine pollutes regardless of its politics." My hope is that Burke is also correct in his later observation that eventually the language of science and technology will function as a critique of itself.

But this is mere hope, and even with its utterance I am made to feel less hopeful.

Around the corner from the museum is the gift shop.

Gift shop?

"Propaganda store" would be more appropriate. For in here is the perfect, corrupting, unhedged bet of video images and space futures that we buy into with a symbol-abusing addict's insensitivity for the logic of symbolic details.

Among the extraordinarily expensive bric-a-brac of space meals (at $4.95 and $7.95 the most exotic form of lean cuisine yet marketed) and space suits ($74.95 buys you what Sears calls a mechanic's outfit and sells for fifty bucks less), bearatroopers and models of the shuttle, are placed Tom Cruise Ray-Bans, Top Gun flight jackets ($289.95), Top Gun caps ($15.95), Cub Cabearabal ($44.95), the *Space Camp* movie ($49.00), and a wide variety of purchasables that strongly suggest that you too can look the part, back home among the less fashionably adorned earthlings.

I ask the right-stuff outfitted counter agent if business is brisk, and she nods. I ask her what is the best-selling item and she points to the Top Gun displays.

I should have known.

Here I am, peering into a mirror with yet another one of those pesky subtexts. In the mirror I too am wearing a cap upon which, in fool's-gold script, reads backwards what frontwards spells United States Space Academy. Backwards it reads YMEDACA ECAPS SETATS DETINU.

Looks like a logical extension of the acronyms evolving from the original issue of NASA, which means, suddenly, that it doesn't look strange or unusual. Just more words to learn, a new grammar in which original meanings and purposes are lost, a grammar, in fact, that begs all questions about meanings and purposes, redefines as its objective not the intelligent conduct of a meaningful life but instead the replacing of that image with another one, a video one, in which thoughts are replaced with moving pictures and feelings are replaced with stereo sound tracks.

To live in this video world is to live in a milieu where opposites attract, where in fact there are only opposites—good/bad, right/wrong, winner/ loser, yes/no, on/off. All the gray area in that mysterious stuff we call gray matter dissolves, and in that dissolve we sacrifice the uniqueness born of creativity and the individuality born of free will to the latent uniformity of a dominant political and bureaucratic obsession.

Like Max Headroom, our body dies but our soul becomes a programmable, likeable, but erasable video image.

A high-ranking research physician, the actual Marcus Welby of NASA who pioneered the medical experiments during the Apollo program, begins his lecture with this definition of the human organism: "From a strictly physiological viewpoint, we are a mass of jelly suspended by a calcium skeleton."

I've never thought of myself that way.

His talk proceeds from this premise in a kind, scientific tone. It is the sort of tone you hope for from a physician sympathetic to your symptoms, a person who has seen about all of it and has managed to retain a sense of humor about those potentials for fear against which life continuously struggles for control.

He continues. "Because of our reliance on earth's gravity for proper bodily functions, in space we have to carry our environment with us.

"To get an idea how important this is we need to understand what happens to humans when they are exposed to a weightless—or more precisely a one-sixth gravity—environment." He turns to his overhead projector and flashes a list on the big screen:

anorexia
nausea
disorientation

sleepiness/sleeplessness
fatigue
restlessness
euphoria
hallucinations
gastrointestinal disturbances
etc.

As he explains each one of these problems I get a distinct feeling for the potential entropic decay of all physiological and neurological systems. Indeed, living in outer space seems less an adventure than a source of foolish pleasure.

"We are vertical animals, not horizontal ones, and our dependence on this posture and the effects of gravity cannot be underestimated. For example, if you spent all day in bed you would be living at the gravity of the moon. And we know some of the problems you would encounter." Another chart:

cardiovascular changes
musculoskeletal changes
endocrine system changes, particularly fluid distribution
psychoneurological problems, particularly perception
closed ecological system dangers, particularly the problem
    of renewing and recycling substances

He then describes the Gemini 7 experiments from which a great deal of his data have been taken because it was one of the very few programs to include consideration of physiological and medical needs in space. For fourteen days prior to the flight, fourteen days during the flight, and fourteen days following the flight, the two astonauts were completely monitored. ("Everything that went into them was taken back out of them, without exception, and sent to the lab. Even their long johns.")

The findings are difficult to talk about and even more difficult to generalize about. However, this physician discusses them in some detail. He found, for example, moderate losses of red cell mass and exercise capacity, postflight orthostatic intolerances, and some loss of bone mineral density, bone calcium, and muscle nitrogen. He also notes the "high metabolic cost of any extravehicular activity," particularly as it was observed in later flights.

During the Apollo program more findings were generated, including severe dehydration and weight loss and the famous case of cardiac arrhythmia caused by one astronaut's failure to eat his prescribed diet. During the three Skylab flights, each one requiring longer exposures to a distinct lack of gravity, so much data was collected that all of it has yet to be analyzed.

(Why? I wonder. That seems improbable to me. Are they hiding something? Are we really not meant for life in space?)

However, the good doctor continues, we do know that prolonged existence in outer space has some dramatic effects on the skeletal system that make the body into a puffy but lengthened and narrowed orb. "You know," he says, musing over his information, "that when we wake up on earth in the morning we are taller, in some cases by almost two inches, than we are when we go to bed at night. That is one way to understand the effects of one-sixth gravity over a period of eight hours."

(Yes, and imagine how you must look after eight days, or eight weeks, or eight months . . .)

The talk then turns its attention to the future, particularly the 250-day planned flight of the shuttle in preparation for the five-year trip to Mars and back. As an audience who has been led gradually to accept the dehumanization and dephysiology that space deterioration brings, we collectively gasp.

"Frankly, if we go through with this mission I predict that due to significant calcium loss leading to failure of skeletal integrity, whoever we send out there will come back a skeletal wreck. Specifically, upon reentering earth's gravitational pull there will likely be multiple fractures of arms, hips, legs— every major bone in the body as a matter of fact. It will be a complete skeletal calamity at 1 gravity."

He continues by pointing out that these problems may be solvable, and suggests that the Soviets are way ahead of us in technology for adapting humans to life in space. At this point he shows us a drawing of the new Soviet space suit that includes interior walls of bungee cords to apply pressure to the bones that may limit calcium deterioration. "Of course, we have little funding for such projects," he laments.

"You know," he continues, "forcing humans to exist in a way contrary to their skeletal definition is like making a monkey stand in a completely upright position. The monkeys we've observed under those conditions go crazy.

"In fact, if you ask me, the whole NASA procedure for selection of astronauts is dead wrong. What we have done is look for people who make good public relations, who look like heroes, but this is all wrong from a physiological perspective.

"The perfect astronaut should be short, obese, with poor muscle tone, and an infinite capacity for boredom. You know, like a college professor."

Not me, doc. Not on your life.

Armed with this sobering intelligence I slowly make my way toward the bubble for my second flight simulation. Thank God this is only a simulation.

On my way over I pause to look around. The air is cool, the sun is bright, birds fly, citizens hold hands and laugh together, and here is sweet gravity providing all that I consider worth having, and which I swear I will never again take for granted.

I get to the simulation room a little late and have to pork myself into an undersized flight suit, giving all the world the impression of a large, blue, walking, talking sausage. I climb aboard the shuttle, take my seat in the orbiter, and watch the video define this experience.

I should point out here that the simulator is a wonderful machine, the sort of thing everybody ought to have our   he backyard for play on rainy days. With a full set of high-tech hydraulics, it simulates (supposedly) the feel of flight, from lift-off to landing, including the drop of the SRBs and the firing of the OMES and the S-turns we must take to get into proper positions. Its sound system also simulates the noise of everything you always wanted to hear from outer space, sans extraterrestials. It makes for a good, even entertaining, ride.

My seat is in the rear of this space bus, a cramped place that disallows movement, particularly if your space suit is tight, as mine is. Phillip the scientist is our commander, and an artist named Spiker is our pilot, and together they suggest what I hope the future of space flight will be, a merging of the sciences and the arts, a transcendence of all that is wrong with the word battles we face because of a lack of understanding predicated by intolerant vocabularies vying for control.

We lift off on schedule and move into orbit with great precision. I cannot quite convey to you how everyone on this flight is caught up in the experience, cannot quite manage to describe the sense of team spirit and common purpose that somehow evolves from this experience. But it does.

I am in charge of opening the hatch and securing the airlock chamber prior to my payload team's move from the orbiter into the lab. To crawl out of my seat is a labor that requires unplugging the earphone jacks of my front-seat colleagues, disconnecting them from contact with earth, and popping a latch on the hatch to let me go by.

We enter the airlock on schedule by crawling through a small hole.

Once inside we fire up the lab, flipping a sequence of toggles and waiting for the entry lights to turn green. My team consists of Jill, a nurse in real life and a fluids scientist in this one, and John, a solar scientist in real life and a scientist in this one, and me, a communications person (as John defines me) in real life and a blue sausage passing for a NASA scientist in this one.

We crawl through the second passage area into the skylab on cue from the principal investigator back on board the orbiter. Here I encounter a problem—the zipper on my too-tight flight suit pops open from the crotch, catches my undershirt in its jaws, and refuses to let me move without exposing those parts of myself I took a vow to reserve for my wife. I therefore declare a "zipper emergency" and ask to speak with the flight director about it.

"Roger. What's the problem?"

"Well, my zipper broke and I'm stuck in the tunnel between the airlock and the lab."

(There is LAUGHTER throughout mission control.) The flight director advises me to find a pair of pliers and zipper myself back up.

"No pliers here, sir."

"Well, do the best you can, soldier."

"Do I have your permission to declare a zipper abort?"

(More howls from my colleagues back on the blue planet.) At this point we lose radio contact due to something I cannot see and have no control over.

I decide to take matters into my own hands and hold the suit closed while dragging myself on my back through the rest of the tunnel and literally dropping over the edge into the lab floor.

John welcomes me aboard and secures the tunnel.

Our experiments begin.

During the next hour I hold my suit shut in the appropriate places while conducting some radio background noise experiments that I do not understand. I also lift a series of weights and record my perception of their relative heaviness, and, thanks to some advice from our resident nurse/scientist, finally manage to reconnect the zipper on my suit and attain some sense of dignity. So pleased am I at the success of this activity that I volunteer to ride the space bike and have my pulse taken, something that back on earth I would find repulsive.

Jill takes my resting pulse and attributes its rate to the heat inside the lab. I attribute it to general bulk and sloth, but say nothing.

After the ride she takes it again and finds that it is much lower. "I may be overweight, but at least I'm in shape," I proclaim. She smiles and tells me it's probably something wrong with the instrument.

Our time in the lab passes quickly and we manage to complete all of our assigned tasks—the first crew to do so!

Back through the tunnel we crawl, once again my zipper aborts, and with hands across my vital organs I manage to retake my seat in the orbiter just as we prepare for reentry.

The visuals provided for this part of the flight are superb. On the screens that pass for the commander and pilot's windows we see the earth come up to greet us, fly over the Banana River, see the easy sway of the trees and the toss of the ocean. As we touch down on the runway we hear the exuberant cries of the mission-control group. We have done it! The *Enterprise* has landed!

"Nice flight, guys," says our simulation director. "That was smooth and as close to perfect as you get."

Alan Bean was the fourth man to walk on the moon. As he stands by the overhead projector prior to his talk, dressed in a blue suit and red tie like a Republican presidential candidate, I flash back to images of moon men and moon suits, an American flag, crackling voices sent back from that distant place to the world that invented its mysteries, made love under its influences, and transformed it, forever, by its human trespass.

Mr. Bean's slide show is a historical account of his own romance on the theme of flight that blends, about half way in, with America's experience of outer space and that lovely orbiting moon. He is a small, witty fellow who tells us that he retired from NASA in 1981 to "collect human stories about man's first adventures in space exploration" and to do his artwork depicting those stories. As an aside he mentions that he had to retire from NASA to do this job because no one at NASA would approve the collecting of human stories as serious work: "They have, you see, no practical engineering value."

As an audience we laugh and warm up to him instantly.

He explains to us, as an image of him as a child squatting next to "the wrong end of a duck" flashes on the screen, that he grew up enchanted with flight, primarily the images of it drawn from John Wayne movies. On his seventeenth birthday he joined the navy, majored in aeronautical engineering at the University of Texas, and eventually made it through flight training. The image changes to a young man squatting next to an F-4.

About this time he began the study of art by enrolling in night school. He shows us a few of his early watercolors, makes a small joke about the framer signing one of them that hangs in his mother's house. About this time, he goes on, he read in *Life* magazine about the Mercury astronauts and he became interested in space flight only because it looked like so much fun. He smiles and recalls that he thought he had the best job in the world flying for the navy, but the idea was that he could have even more fun flying for NASA.

Seeing the first launch convinced him. At this point he shows us a vivid photograph of the Apollo 12 on the launch pad and tries to convey to us the awe and sense of beauty it inspired in him as he walked out to it in the crisp early morning of the moon flight. He explains to us that the reason the moonship looks so sparkling and so white is because the fuel tanks are cold and the wind that whips across their surfaces makes ice that reflects the morning sun. He tells us that he remembers very clearly hearing, from 360 feet up in the space capsule, the thin ice break, slide, and eventually crash against the ground.

"That was when it dawned on me that we really were going to the moon this morning," he says quietly. Then: "At about T minus three seconds when the rockets fired and the missile began shaking I remember thinking that maybe we shouldn't go," but (here he flashes up a shot of the launch vehicle breaking away from the pad), "it was too late then."

This brings the house down.

"People ask me what it's like to pull away from the pad. They see the smoke and flames on television and figure it must be incredible. It isn't, really. It's like pulling away from a stoplight in a sports car. What you have to understand is that you are 360 feet up and all that rumble and noise takes time to reach you. You can move around, you aren't thrown back into your seat. It's very smooth. What I remember thinking about is that now I know how a bone feels in a dog's mouth.

"About one and a half minutes into the flight we were struck by lightning, some of the electronics went out, but by then it didn't matter." He puts a view of the earth from outer space before us, talks about it, puts up another one of the earth from the surface of the moon.

"Then we were there. From the surface of the moon you can see deserts and oceans, but not continents. The earth is a blue Easter egg [my sentiments exactly!], the only beautiful sight in the sky."

For the next few minutes we see more examples of his moon art, each one described. He tells us that he took up his astronaut pin and one of the first things he did on the moon was throw it into the Surveyor crater. It was then he realized that even his footprints would last twenty million years.

During this period of reminiscence he tells us, against the backdrop of his painting *Tiptoing on the Ocean of Storms*, that you could run a marathon on the moon and never get tired, that when he dropped tools they never hit the ground, that when they were driving around in the space car they would hit a boulder and become airborne and stay up there in the air with their wheels spinning.

"People want to know what it felt like to be on the moon. Well, you know you are an alien, an earth person. You don't belong there." He tells us about the famous picture of John Young jumping up and saluting the flag, and how afterwards his partner tried the same thing, believing he could jump even higher, but lost his balance and fell over on his back. "NASA was mad about that one," he grins, "because if the suit had ripped open he would have died." Right, no PR value in that.

"We had some fun up there. I remember walking over to the satellite to do some repairs. The manuals were strapped onto our forearms, and we were supposed to do the repair sequence according to their instructions. Well, somebody had taped *Playboy* bunnies into the checklist and there we were on the moon!

"Then, after we lifted off from the moon Pete Conrad moved us to the dark side so I could have a chance to fly the machine. NASA never knew about this," he chuckles. "You do that sort of thing because it's important to have a little fun."

He shows us a slide with the sun eclipsed by the earth and mentions, almost under his breath, "Only three people have ever seen this sight."

Back on earth, "The first thing I remember was seeing water move, feeling the wind move. It was a great feeling. Home again."

The second space experience for Mr. Bean was the time he spent in Skylab, and he shows us a series of slides depicting life inside the ship: getting a haircut with a vacuum cleaner, taking a bath ("you just reach out and grab a handful of water"). He explains to us that there is no body odor in space but lots of gas.

We see the astronauts looking out the window and I think I know why.

He explains to us that this is one of the most exciting things you can do in space, look back at the earth, pick out things, watch the world go by. He tells us about one of his buddies who yelled, "Communist!" every time they shot by the Soviet Union.

He then shows us a headline from one of those newsstand tabloids that shout the incredible, the unbelievable, at you. This one confirms that the astronauts saw UFOs in outer space, and he explains that this is just not true. "They sent a reporter who asked us about it, and we told him, and the next day this headline appeared."

Toward the end of his presentation Mr. Bean showed us the *Challenger* explosion as depicted by a NASA artist. Oddly enough, this is the first time in the whole of our space camp experience that the *Challenger* accident has been mentioned. Mr. Bean explains how the accident occurred in exact detail, surprising really, and shares with us his view that improvements have been made and the next shuttle flight will get us back on track.

The formal presentation ends and the questions begin.

A person on the front row wants to know if we should cooperate with the Russians. Mr. Bean says, "Absolutely. One thing you learn up there is that this is a very small planet, but it's all one piece and it's all we've got. I don't know if we can trust them, but I do know we must work with them to find out."

Someone wants to know if all the old astronauts get together and talk about their experiences. "Sure, some of us do. But not all of us." He says that last week, for example, he was signing prints in Ohio when a woman walked up to him—he didn't recognize her—and began speaking as if she knew him. Finally, she said, "You don't know who I am, do you?"

"No," he replied honestly, "I'm afraid I don't."

"I'm Jan Armstrong," she said.

"My God, Jan! I haven't seen you or Neil for fifteen years!"

One thing led to another and she invited him out to their farm for dinner. He told us that Neil Armstrong, the first man to walk on the moon, retired from NASA to a 360-acre dairy farm near Lebanon, Ohio.

"It's a wonderful old place," Mr. Bean tells us, "a 150-year old farmhouse that is really nice. But the odd thing is that when you walk inside there is not one thing, not one reminder, that this is the house of the man who first walked on the moon." Perhaps his neighbors, who know him only as a farmer, don't even make the connection.

This clearly troubles Mr. Bean.

"His wife runs the farm, though, and Neil owns a computer software company."

I am thinking: Imagine *that*.

We graduate in a wings-and-certificate ceremony that lasts nearly an hour. We are tired campers, ready to go home.

I don't remember much about it except that my wife came in to see it and there were television cameras on the high-ranking university official. There was the "Right Stuff" award which was given to a science-fiction freak from New York State who gave a short speech about writing to our congressmen every six months to support the space program. Earlier in the day he had mentioned to me that he planned to ask for money to "continue this experience" but I explained to him that such a call for action with this group would probably not do any good.

Then it was over.

Back on my farm, out in the quiet of the countryside, I stand for a while on my own back porch and stare at the moon.

It is a large, yellow presence that seems to sit suspended against the outer limbs of Homer Bright's apple trees. My retrievers are with me, and my wife is out at the barn tending the horses. As a graduate of the United States Space Academy I feel as if I have come back to earth after three days in space, and believe it is my duty to capture the essence of this experience here, and now.

Nothing happens.

Later in the night I wake to hear our local owl calling, and there is gravity that makes possible a nice little breeze.

I still want to be eloquent, but it is almost midnight and just not in me.

All that is right now is enough. More than.

I am thinking: Let the moon be, for it is pretty. Let the stars alone, for they do not mean us any harm. Delight in the deluxe of gravity, do not try to escape it. There is work yet to be done in this garden, on this blue planet, this tortured and heavenly place.

5

Articles of Faith

But meanings can only be "stored" in symbols:
a cross, a crescent, or a feathered serpent.
Such religious symbols, dramatized in rituals
or related in myths, are felt somehow to sum up,
for those for whom they are resonant, what is known
about the way the world is, the quality of the
emotional life it supports, and the way one ought
to behave while in it.

—Clifford Geertz, "Ethos, World View,
and the Analysis of Sacred Symbols"

PROCESSIONAL

University Drive is alive with traffic, bordered with signs. Its increasingly crowded four lanes and many accidents are but one testament to the ongoing population explosion that defines Huntsville's current prosperity. Since the advent of the Star Wars research program and the bidding wars for space station contracts, our city has again boomed. Traffic has never been this bad, business has never been better.

Everything counts when everything is changing.

Because I spend a good deal of my daily commuting time on University Drive I have witnessed this era's growth, particularly the quick expansion westward toward the nouveau affluent suburb of Madison, with more than a passing interest. Fields that were plowed and where cotton was grown last year are this year sown with the fescue lawns of new housing, and the housing is already occupied. Everywhere there are new subdevelopments, and with them come new business opportunities—convenience stores, gas stations, retail outlets, fast-food chains, and recently even faster-food chains—little rectangular buildings with dual windows and no inside seating, places where bucks and burgers and fries can be exchanged to satisfy people hungry to rejoin the traffic on University Drive.

I wonder about the meanings of all this movement. For example, what does it mean when a community thrives on fast and faster food? Where

93

even the better restaurants flaunt the prepackaged and the precooked? What is it that we are, as a community, really hungry for?

There is also the mystery that is called "the new mall." This is the long-awaited Madison Square Super Mall, recently opened, around which have blossomed in the past two years smaller shopping centers and outlets, generic doctor-in-a-box no-waiting clinics, food stores, discount clothing chains, sporting goods stores, music stores, and seven—count them—new-car dealerships (Chevrolet, Hyundai, Acura, Dodge/Chrysler, Plymouth, Jeep/Eagle, and Nissan/Mercedes Benz).

This is happening along a strip of highway on which pace a small but steadily increasing lost army of the homeless, the Winn-Dixie daytime cart pushers who drag the streets for the salvageable and at night sleep under the overpasses, our very own street people who remind the civic leaders that something must be done. This message appears on the television screen, usually during our one annual snowstorm, and then, like the snow, is gone again. The story changes, but the homeless and the boom of the business expansion remain.

Peacefully they coexist, for now. I used to be able to count the number of homeless cart pushers on one hand, even knew two of them by name. Now I can't count the number, and I do not want to know their names. Whatever is going on here is going on also inside of me.

I understand growth, and the Profit Motive, but what do these symbols tell us about ourselves beyond the obvious glitter of our neon desire to consume, and the absence of everything when we fail to? What is it, specifically, that we are consuming?

I need to look into this, into me.

Take myself and my surroundings seriously. Apply what I have learned about reading. Find the story.

This is, of course, taking place in the City of Progress, a city and its suburbs full of people and their signs. A nice place—very nice—to live and work, really.

Commercial jets, this time, come screaming across the sky.

TEXT AND PRE-TEXT

The sign on the door says simply "Discount Records."

I have lately been rereading too much Stanley Fish and so this sign and I become a semiotic situation, a text with a pretext, something mutually created in the odd never-not of the ever-present now. Should

I read it: *Don't pay any attention to records, all ye who enter here?* Or should it mean: *Records here are cheaper than you would expect?* Or how about: *We only discount records in here, and you have to pay full retail on tapes, CDs, movies, and so on?*

Too much Fish, obviously. All Fished out.

For everyone else the sign is what it is, which is more and less than what it stands for. "More" because it isn't just a store that sells records; it is more importantly an invitation to author a cultural experience—to actually *discount* records (in the sense that means "forget")—and to instead open the door not just to a store, but to an adventure with an identity. "Less" because to look for the reason given for said cultural event—to peruse or to purchase Discounted Records—is to see only the negative of a technicolor movie, where what clearly appears to be absent is all you think you miss.

It is the more and less of the sign itself that attracts us, its inducing of interpretations of self, a consumer twist of Walt Whitman's symbolically rich phrase "democratic vistas." This is the America we all move in and out of, stores with images of self for sale, dramas with costumed salespersons and beliefs about price, an America called Retail.

Come inside.

"Can I help you?" says a man named Turner whose name tag identifies him as the store manager.

Turner is smiling. He sports a fashionably trimmed Viennese psychiatrist's beard. What sort of "help" is he actually offering? Is my self in such obvious trouble? Or is it that I have come in here for self-ish reasons, maybe just to look around, to shop comparatively, without the legitimate intention to purchase the merchandise and all it suggests? If this is the case, Turner's question may be an attempt to stimulate my latent desire to consume.

"Do you have the film *Stranger than Paradise?*" I ask.

Turner reflects on it—this is his moment to strut and fret upon the stage—so he really does *reflect* on it: his eyes roll upward, he squints, he bites his lower lip, shakes his head "no." It is a narratively valid performance, a display of honest effort on the job. Turner can be trusted. "We should have it in the next shipment," he confides. "I can hold it for you."

"That would be nice." By which I mean, "Please do, because I want to see it, experience it, before anyone else can do so." The future with me and the movie, a movie I've never seen and have only once heard about, flashes through my head. There is a young, unidentified, ruined blonde actress in it, there is a cheap hotel room with a brass lamp, there is a car outside, and maybe it's Florida . . .

"Consider it done." Turner scribbles a note on a small white pad he keeps in his shirt pocket, like a doctor writing a prescription for a controlled substance. "Since you're here anyway," he continues, "why not look around? You might find something you like." The "since" of his sentence troubles me, "since" denoting time and "because" properly denoting reason, the effect of which is to suggest that I have been without an identity since the last time I was here, time and being enjoying a sudden, inexplicable Heideggerian *entendre*.

I follow Turner's orders.

PERSONS AND THINGS

I never really enter the same store twice. Once I am past the cash register, a symbol that never moves or changes its meaning, each experience of Discount Records is brand new, an adventure in consuming.

The stereo sound this hour features Wolfgang Amadeus Mozart's *Divertimenti* as played by the Academy of St. Martin's-in-the-Fields. Members of the audience this hour include one pair of teenage girlfriends, each one trying to outblow the other in a purple bubble-gum contest, to out-hair the other one with equally indescribable masses of reddish-brown hair, each one wearing this season's uniform two layers of pastel summer sweaters that are manufactured loose, long, and always large enough to let one shoulder and the strap of a white sleeveless undershirt show through. They are examining the covers of aerobic dancing records, talking about how much money their boyfriends will make as electrical engineers.

In the back a pale young man with a golden earring hides the color of his eyes behind sunglasses. He pins buttons to his shirt to express his feelings: SS-DD (Same Shit–Different Day); Life's a Beach; and two scenes from covers of heavy metal albums, one with a cross bludgeoned with daggers, the other a pale, made-up-for-MTV star face. He just stands there, stands there staring at the joining of two corners at the end of the store, maybe projecting himself into the slick red-and-white poster image of Tina Turner, maybe not.

By the video racks are two adult males, unmarried or maybe recently divorced, both middle-aged and overweight, both making a scary attempt to look young again. They sport leather ties (one white, one blue) and pastel "Miami Vice" jackets (one blue, one yellow). The white-and-blue heavier of the two holds a brand-new copy of *American Ninja* while his blue-and-yellow self-suffering sidekick performs an excited oral history of old James Bond classics. Their faces are really having a work out, all the animated tics and jerks of epidermal spa-tans stretching the limits of skin, two sources of self-doubt wearing out the welcome of self-expression.

A little farther down the rack stands a well-dressed working woman, also wearing sunglasses, trying to decide between *Young Sherlock* and *Santa Claus—The Movie*. A *Jagged Edge* box is tucked under her arm with the words sticking out. She doesn't look like she is enjoying this. Unlike most customers she doesn't attempt eye contact, not even eye contact of the brief, fleeting, "I'm-interesting-but-you're-not" variety. There are no gold rings on her left hand, which confirms my suspicions about the point of her sunglasses, the ages of her children, and a certain attitude toward men somehow suggested by her choice of movies.

Up front, working the cash register, is Turner. Usually he is assisted by one of three employees, each one a strategic choice of image. There is a young black woman whose name tag reads "Cheryl" and who laughs more than she talks; a young, deeply tanned Caucasian man who displays a bush of black chest hair from the top half of Hawaiian shirts. He gives the impression of a cool, laid-back dude. His eyes never fully look at you, engage you, as if to do so would make you into something more than a customer, perhaps a person as real and exciting as himself.

The third assistant is a permanent part-timer, a sporty young WASPy woman who plays the full-time ditz, looks like a late night, and tells customers she is a math whiz. And then there is Turner, at one time a serious film and literature student who could not seem to complete term papers, a friendly guy who has held on to his very first car, a green and obviously dangerous Vega, a man before thirty who seems to have come to grips with the drift of his life, an image of self-control.

Divertimenti ends.

In its place Cheryl chooses the new Bananarama album and turns up the sound just a bit, as if a subtle increase in volume is important to this record, an emblem of a memory, maybe, a mental image that comes equipped with sound. She begins to dance.

She dances from the first to the last of the music, moving herself in a kind of rhythmic semicircle among the new stacks of albums piled in non-neat rows on the floor. Her task is to nonsort and nonplace them, a task she nonaccomplishes without much thought while continuing to indulge herself in dance. I am reminded of the line from *The Sound of Music* spoken by the father of the family Von Trapp: "Activity gives the illusion of a life full of purpose."

The door opens and two twentyish black women enter, each one stylishly attired in this generation's version of tight Capri pants and Danskin tops. They approach Cheryl, call her name, heavily accenting and dragging out the last syllable until it becomes a whole mood, a sign more of the recognition of an aspect of self than of the whole person. She never misses a beat, though, keeps on moving, the interruptions of friends little more than a temporary accompaniment, two new instruments to blend into her performance of the dance.

What strikes me as unusual is not her ability to dance while talking to customers, but the fact that she doesn't stop when they approach her. It reminds me of a friend of mine who sings in her car every morning on the way to work. When she stops for a red light and sees someone staring at her, she doesn't stop singing, she just sings louder.

In both cases there is a sense of self on display that realizes its image, accepts it, and actively chooses to live in it. I'd like to climb in their ears and see what goes on inside their heads, move into their bloodstreams and see how it feels to live that way. It's probably the only way to test my notions about what it means.

THE WHITE, MIDDLE-CLASS SOUL OF THE NEW CONSUMER

I know that every generation has a loosely developed but commonly understood celebrity image of itself, images that go back to long before Mary, Christ, and Judas. Each generation seems to define those alternative human experiences of self in images—facial expressions, costumes, music, and behavior—during its adolescence, and then carries the images into the later reaches of adulthood, when nostaglia at first deepens, then clouds the remembrances, then forces a struggle with the idea that they may in fact be irrelevant, given the larger, more final examinations in life.

I know this about as well as everyone else does, but something has changed, and changed only recently. Daniel Boorstin got at a big part of it when he described one influence of the media on the human psyche as the destruction of the myth of the hero (someone who is known for doing a good deed) and the construction of the myth of the celebrity (someone who is "well known for being well known"). Yet there is still something missing, something beyond the birth of celebrities that induces this common desire to live in images of self that are not our self. Certainly the media is responsible for creating the stereotypes and for defining who it is fashionable these days to be.

But I believe the root cause is in us rather than around us, an evolutionary step off into a symbolic wonderland of possibilities, the sort of step a schizophrenic takes when there is increased excitement at the synapses, the sort of step a culture takes when it discovers its own ineffable sources of entropic decay. What makes this historical period different, if not unique, is that as long as we separate our symbolic selves from our real selves in ways that can be consumed, bought and paid for with cash or the imaginary cash we euphemistically refer to as "credit cards," then the exchange of symbols of money for symbols of self is viewed as not merely an equitable exchange, but an exchange that should be culturally endorsed. "How much did it cost you?" is a question that has developed a whole new set of meanings.

Furthermore, what we seem to be endorsing is a self thick with temporary and transient facades, a blurring of the architecture of dress, decor, discourse, and deportment that carries with it a blurring of the real and the imagined foundations of self. Out of this blur of symbolic possibilities, symbolic inducements increasingly pass for good reasons, and symbolic attachments increasingly appear to be the source of true emotions. The idea is not merely to display symbols that identify ourselves with celebrities, but to justify our behavior, our flaunting of the self-as-celebrity as ours because we own not the same soul, but the same symbols as the celebrity.

Still this flaunting of self-as-celebrity, and this lack of embarrassment about the flaunting, suggests that the facade is not felt as a facade, which further suggests that what is known to be true about the self in these self-presentations is a truth whose origins are sort of Platonic fictions. As Plato/Socrates argued, this is not the real world, but the phenomenal world, a world of images and half-truths. There are real and knowable truths, ideal forms that can be apprehended because we once knew them when our souls flew in that other world. That is why we are attracted to them, why they seem "true" and "natural" to us when they are put into words. And to get at these ideal forms of truth again we need to acquire the philosopher's methods, chief among them the ability to ask questions aimed at getting back to that original source of truth.

For this group of citizens of the phenomenal world the ideal forms and knowable truths exist on television, in videos, in stereo, on film, and between the covers of fashionable magazines. Their souls once knew them (how else can you describe the influences of those media on children's minds?) and are now once again attracted to them in ways that seem both "true" and "natural." And because media is a consumer-oriented medium, the questions these philosophers quickly learn to ask are questions not of truth, goodness, and beauty, but of consuming, living, and wanting, questions whose answers are arrived at through the purchase of images.

Ours may not be the first generation for whom the soul is for sale or at least has a price, but it may be the first to buy into the idea that what feeds the soul is not substance, but symbols, not questioning the meanings of life, but instead seeking to ignore them.

Writers have for some time now known that fiction can create its own world and the rules for living in it, a fact of prose and film that almost goes without saying.

But what happens when these fictional worlds become our living reality, when our beliefs about self, about relationships, about politics, and about organizations are as easily derived from the world of make-believe as they are from the world we make up as we go along? Maybe the issue should be stated differently: What happens when there is no longer any important difference between fiction and nonfiction, between what is real and what is imagined, between images of self based on who and what we are and images of self based on fantasies?

This is what happens when a culture is built on the selling and buying of products, and the products become interchangeable components of our imaginary selves. This is what is learned from the lessons of marketing those products, lessons of the need to appeal to surface identities, to visual and aural images, by exciting the senses that can convince us to buy into figments of our own cultural imaginations, into characters in stories, stories with stars.

Now as anyone who has ever listened to a good storyteller knows, every good story has a beginning, some development, and an ending. Maybe this is why it is difficult to leave a retail store empty-handed. There is a failure of self that is associated with the failure to consume, to make just one more purchase, to complete the narrative of the ideal transaction.

For the sales staff this failure can be a source of wolfish one-upspersonship ("Didn't have the money to buy what you really wanted, eh?") that speaks to the attitude they convey, an attitude of a superior that suggests a close identification with the images of self offered for sale. If you have ever gotten the feeling that salespeople act like they owned it, then you have witnessed this identification. For the consumer who has failed to consume, who walks out empty-handed, there is a lingering sense of loss, but it is a loss that gives way to a renewed sense of adventure. After all, there are many stores, and many stories, out there in the land of disposable identity.

The personal narrative that begins with the innocent "Where should I go next?" can quickly develop into a serious, complex character plot. From the vantage of a single store, and its incomplete story, there are novel possibilities just across the street, in a larger narrative structure known as the mall.

I never leave Discount Records, I abandon it. My relationship doesn't end, it evolves. So does my identity, so does my story.

GOING TO THE MALL

From the earliest anthropological and archaeological data about humans we have, we know our need to organize activities comes with the desire to organize territories for the enactment of those activities. Think *communitas,* city-state, nation, empire, world.

Perhaps this is a way to explain the rise of shopping malls, which are more than enclosed shopping centers, and where what goes on within them is more than the sale of merchandise. For a shopping mall is also an image ripe for our time, an image of an ideal community where temperature, humidity, and behavior are almost always perfectly controlled, and where the appropriate metaphor for describing what is experienced there may well be fiction. For a mall is a cultural community unto itself, a place where strategy, money, and imagination induce dramas committed to narratives of self. For self-seeking consumers in Huntsville such a surround is found at the Madison Square Mall.

You find malls like this one everywhere in America, because shopping malls are essentially alike, although every one of them fosters a thematic appeal that is meant to be unique. Jerry Jacobs, a professor at Syracuse University, points out there are well over twenty-three thousand malls in America, and what characterizes the mall experience is that they are the only places that look like this regardless of where they are or who works there. He writes: "To add to the physical sense of sameness one experiences upon [sic] the mall, there is the question of the kinds of people who go to malls and what they do when they get there. . . . Unlike the variety of people one might encounter in a downtown area, one does not encounter vagrants, drunks, prostitutes, street people, ex-mental patients, the retarded, or many blacks or ethnics in suburban mall settings" (*The Mall*, 13).

It is the univeral McDonald's or perhaps the old IBM uniformed, monotone effect that ensures us that foolish consistency, even if the hobgoblin of small minds, is the basis of a decidedly white, middle-class desire to consume. It is the promise of what Kenneth Burke calls "consubstantiality," that perfect union made out of symbols of transcendent identification, that welcomes us into the deepest sources of consumer satisfaction.

The purposefulness of the place is evident in the entrance sign:

> No Overnight Parking
> No Cruising
> No Soliciting

This is, obviously, a sign with many intended meanings, some only slightly more ironic than others.

For example, who would want to park overnight here? A consumer whose love of the mall object or its contents prevents her or him from leaving its side? Only rarely so. More likely it refers to the plight of the stranded narrator, the customer whose vehicle breaks down in the lot, fails to start, or is empty of the necessary fluids, a vehicle that refuses to respond even to the vulgar threats and warnings made against it by its driver, or against its driver by the other passengers, each with a story rich with individuality. It is, in short, a warning for the owner of a potentially dangerous vehicle whose flagrant neglect for the well-being of the vehicle and disrespect for the law of the lot may force the indignity, delay, and inconvenience of towing.

Cruising? No cruising, either? How could this be when every mother's son and daughter among us claims the right to wander around in malls, some of us until we require medical assistance? There is no necessary intent to purchase evident in our behavior as mall walkers. Part of the social contract here is the right to "shop around," which means, taken literally, the right to wander around aimlessly staring into windows, making up stories about other people's eyes. No, the cruising that is forbidden here must refer to parking lot cruising, the vagrant, "Hey, *baby*, who's your *daddy?*" cruising that suggests a night to remember based on the need to forget.

Soliciting is also forbidden, according to the sign. *Of what sort?* is the important question. After all, the purpose of a mall is the solicitation of business, which is nothing more or less than the open, public expression of a hidden, private desire. If this community means to forbid soliciting, it must be soliciting of a styleless or kinky kind, which, in this end of the twentieth century, must refer to the unholy trinity of politics, religion, or sex you have to pay for. For those sources of identity you must select from the menus of mass communication: the telephone or the television, the newspaper or magazine. However, all of these sources of socially unacceptable gratification can be bought inside the mall, so the intention to forbid solicitation of even these scandalous sources of semiotic relationships are not entirely out of reach to those who make a common practice of telling stories about how they get around signs.

Anyway, the sign is small. You only see it if you walk into the parking lot from any of its entrances, which is appropriate because no one who has to walk to the mall really belongs there. It is a sign meant for the narratively poor of society, those with fixed, nondisposable identities, the class of people who never enter malls because they don't drive the right cars or own the right clothes, the class of people who will never hold an American Express card, the class of people who wouldn't care whether or not a store was having a sale because the price of admission, of just walking in there, moving up to a counter, asking for help, *and getting that look in return*, is too high a price to ever pay to another human being.

An Interlude in Another World

There are stores, and older, mostly abandoned malls, for these people. These are the various "marts" and "discount warehouses" that increasingly populate America, places that seldom share more than two short syllables for a name, as if the air to say more about them would be like an unfair tax against those who shop there. These are the white-walled places that make your hair reek of cotton candy and titillate the scent receptors in your nose with the underwhelming aromas of margarine-flavored popcorn before you get to the first discount counter, stores that post a guard at the front door to check your packages for contraband, stores that always feature the large invisible VOICE to announce hourly specials under the red or blue or green light, a consumer-sensitive salesgod who can lead you to the path of purchaseness and who restoreth your identity as a smart shopper.

These are the stores that offer more for less for people who feel that way about themselves in a circus surround where the way you paint your face and do your hair, the car you drive, and the clothes you wear represent accurately the roles you are enacting in society. There is no need to appeal to the imagination here because there is too little time for that. The world of these consumers is a world of work and toil and tradition; life is real and limited by the vocabulary of the necessary, the decent, and the right.

There are divisions of purchase in retail America our forefathers should have feared. This is a retail America that, on one hand, offers freedom that, when carried into the mainstream of a consumer-based culture, makes the purchase of identity and participation in a story more appealing than life itself. Yet in this same land, life itself sets that freedom off-limits to all those who aren't in the mainstream because it comes with a commonly understood social responsibility to display forms of, well, cultural literacy. Compare the crowds at the marts to those at the mall: not just their faces, their clothing, their places in the commonweal, but the stories they tell and the words they use to tell them. Here is the true source of our new national problem, a retail problem that is really a problem of identity and the vocabulary of identity, about choosing how and where to buy, and about how we feel about ourselves when we buy.

It is easy to leave the other side of shopping, the marts and warehouses of America.

Easy. Easy, especially if you don't really feel that you belong there, and going there in the first place was motivated solely by the price of the product not the worth of your soul. To drive away is to shed a mask that identifies you with a way you would rather not be, and a feeling about being that seems cheap, or poor, or that simply lacks imagination. This is admittedly an odd thought, given that most of the products in these stores are the same ones that you find at the super mall, just less expensive.

But perhaps not. It is seldom the price of the product alone that massages our ego, appeals to our id, or sides with our superego. If that was all there was to the experience of retail in America there would no good reason to pay more for the narrative quest inherent to the mall experience.

The Feeling upon Entering the Mall

To live in retail America is to purchase more than a product; it is to identify oneself with the environment, to surround the presentation of oneself with images that speak to the worth of the effort of self-display.

On one level it may be seen as a way to participate in the display, to show oneself to be the veritable image of the image itself. On another level it may be to participate in a deep-play narrative dramatization of a more perfect life for people whose lives can no longer be spent enacting the rituals and routines of the merely phenomenal. And on yet another level it may be a way to exercise a sense of self-worth by surrounding that self with symbols of material worth.

Regardless of the reading given to this text, there is one unifying theme, one central statement at the core of our consumer culture. That statement speaks of the need to become one with an appeal that is more appealing, and ultimately more satisfying, than the ordinary reality of *just buying a product*. The mall, then, is the source of a powerful appeal to our collective middle-class imagination that not only makes possible, but actually markets, the ideal nature of narrative consumer fiction.

To go shopping at the Madison Square Mall is to gain a class-conscious sense of a questing self, a self searching, ultimately, for that one moment of true feeling that combines the experience of purchase with the owner-ship of a product, and the ownership of that product with an environmentally induced identity symbolic of imagined, actualizing selfhood. By purchasing it you buy bragging rights, an adventure to be told, and in the retelling, relived. So it is important not only *what* you bought, but *where* you bought it. And for close friends and maybe spouses, what gets underscored is neither the product nor the place, but how you felt about the conquest as it happened, step by step, episode by episode, from the beginning unto the end.

THE PARISIAN'S POINT OF VIEW

Nowhere is this truth easier to recognize than at the heart of fashion in a fashion-conscious mall, its best (highest status) fashion department store—in this case, Parisian's.

Whoever markets this store knows this to be true. For example, the store's jingle singers put it this way: *"Get the Parisian's point of view! It's in everything we do! We're the store for special people! With the Parisian's point of view!"*

What is "the Parisian's point of view?"

Joan Didion, an author whose sensitivity to repetitive statements and restatements of the repetitive statements makes a strong argument for the common form of the fashionable among contemporary Americans, says somewhere in a novel that "style is character." I think that whatever the Parisian's point of view might be, she's got a line on it. What we have here is a desire to communicate the ideal forms of beauty in a culture that, as Ellen Bersheid and Elaine Walster put it, too often confuses, or at least substitutes, "the beautiful for the true." What we have here at Parisian's is a repetitive statement rich with rhetorical invitations to possess fashionable containers for the self in the hope of becoming one with the implied magic of the image contained. This is the America of mass-produced style, a place where once you go in the only thing that has to be real is your credit card.

Look at the architecture, the design of this container that is what it tries to do to you. If you could slice away the top of the super mall (a "double dumbbell" design, by the way, according to Horace Carpenter's work on mall architecture) to see the inside from above, Parisian's would look like a large, octagonal, female organ with an elevated centerpiece made out of three televisions (all on the same soap opera channel), expensive chocolates (all from the same imported source), and RED repetitions of the same deep RED amplified shade RED of the theme color RED. *Yes! I said Yes I will Yes!* From this top-down vantage I am certain you would see most of the activity, the pulsing promenades of the players in this drama, teasing the edges of the centerpiece for a while before making their final assault on the thing itself.

Parisian's is a two-storied structure, with the elevated centerpiece located midway between the stories. The top floor is mostly male gear, with David's Cookies and some infant wear toward the rear. The bottom floor is all female gear, with separate counters for various brand-name cosmetics (Clinique, Charles of the Ritz, etc.) and designer clothing.

This traditional arrangement—men on top, women on bottom—contributes also to the traffic patterns of the store. Men learn to enter Parisian's from the top. Women mostly do not. If my language here seems derived gratuitously from the metaphors of sex, it is because it is meant to. Parisian's—from the implications of its French name to the way it solicits your business—is all revved up with carnal implications. The effect it creates is one of a giant, two-story, sweetly scented bedroom and eatery populated by fashionable dolls who have acquired the Parisian's point of view.

The point of view, derived fundamentally from a postmodern turn in the streams of sexual consciousness, a turn that attracts the already attracted, promises knowledge for those who already know, encourages what can best be described as an *attitude*. If you read no further than the covers of *Vogue* or *Glamour* or *Cosmo* at the grocery checkout counters, you've seen it expressed in the unnnaturally light dark bright look in too-blue eyes, and in the slightly puckered pouts of the sensuous too-red mouths the cover girls own when photographed. This look reflects control over its delicious weakness, emotional control under the spell of a certain but mysterious authority, the effect of which is to create, with nothing more or less powerful than that look captured, an image that demands to be had.

If you read beyond the covers of those popular rhetorics of public undress, you discover the ways and means of creating the cover-girl effect, and if you move up to the cosmetics and fashion counters of Parisian's you find examples, in the form of persons, happy to advance their Crackerjack surprise-in-the-box secrets of beauty.

The Counter as Statement, the Clerk as Cultural Icon

As Kenneth Burke and, more recently, Jacques Derrida have taught us, symbols have the equipotential to unite and divide, attract and repel, share in and exclude, those who respond to them as symbols.

Ellen Bersheid and Elaine Walster, following their own conceptual instincts about the symbolic appeals of beauty, have found that we have a sense of how attractive we are as symbols. We exist, in our own minds, at a fixed point on a relative scale, the all-American universal scale of one to ten, and we seek out others whose daily numbers match or at the very least come close to our own. Hence, we may admire or appreciate the high rollers in this numbers game, but we are actually attracted to ones closer to our own self-assessment.

These ideas help explain the feelings I have about counter clerks in stores such as Parisian's. There seems to be a range of high-medium to medium-perfect beauty represented here, a full range of 8s through the low 9s, representing numbers just a little bit higher than the routine consumers who shop here, living testimonies, I guess, to what can happen to you if you follow their advice about the products. Hence, the counter clerk at Parisian's represents a cultural icon of sorts, a symbol of the logic behind what is being sold as merchandise: a cultural fantasy/belief about beauty-as-product as major premise, a seductive icon embodying symbolically that fantasy/belief as minor premise, and if you accept these premises as being real, then the only valid conclusion you can reach causes you to reach for the cash or credit card of your choice. Here is the enthymemic basis for our purchase decisions, where what we are buying is the right to feel an emotional high with narrative high fidelity.

If you watch what happens when a customer walks up to a counter, the counter itself being a barrier to actual physical contact that is also a place to display and to touch the goods, you will probably see a choice being made, a choice that is one of identification with, and division from, images of self-reflected beauty. Regardless of the sex or gender of the customer, the same rule seems to apply: we try to do business with those who most resemble what we want ourselves to be. If we violate the rule, seek out someone too far above or below our range of perceived beauty, then we are suggesting that either we don't need to obey the rules or that we believe that images aren't real. Take either road in this community where image is King as well as Everything, and you will be judged, as communication rules theorist Susan Shimanoff puts it, "mad or bad." When we break the rules of well-understood codes, we gamble with the social outcomes, which is to say we roll against the numbers in a big, aggressive, interpersonal way.

However, Bersheid and Walster did find that there are cases where these rules can be violated and yet the violation is ignored: Older, richer, more powerful but less attractive men or women can induce the cooperation of younger, poorer, less powerful but more attractive women or men, where equity is achieved by cashing in youth and beauty for money and status. In our culture it is okay to gamble with the rules when you can afford to rewrite them. The cultural rhythms between beauty and money apparently dance to a different beat than other dancers do.

Perhaps this is why, in the most capitalistic culture on this champion planet, we endorse emphatically a cult of physical beauty. It is physical beauty—when every other argument about the mind or manners has been made—that is the best and surely the fastest way to advance a fortune. Without doing much headwork, the formulas for beauty surround us, their images dance with or against us in daylight and darkness, no matter who or where we are or what we do.

This is why, I think, we spend in America as much each year on cosmetics and soap as we do on nuclear weapons.

The World According to Cosmetics

"How can I help you!" she exclaims with the Parisian's point of view.

Is she suggesting that I should be anxious to receive all the help her counter can provide? Or is she just excited? "I'm not sure," I respond.

"Good!" she says, perking right up like a terrier.

"Good?"

"Yes! Good!" She flashes a BIG WHITE SMILE, bats her unnatural eyelashes in my general direction. This must be part of what they learn to become Parisian girls. "This gives me a chance to try out our new customer survey on you!"

Go with it, remember? "Okay," I say, about as tentatively as I know how to.

"Great!" She is coming on in a heated rush on every word. She must do aerobics. "First question!"

"First question," I repeat.

"Is your skin dry?" She doesn't sound happy. "Oh, I forgot, you are supposed to rank this on a scale of one to ten."

Naturally.

"In places," I respond, honestly. "Or if I work all day outside in the wind."

"Is that a five?"

"Okay, a five then." I lean forward, trying to see the questionnaire.

"Next question!" She huffs, SMILES, reads. "Do you take more than one shower or bath a day?"

"Only in the summer."

"Is that a five, too?" She looks up at me with the BIG EYES.

"I don't think so. This is summer, so on your scale it would correspond to about an eight, maybe a nine. However, if this was December and you asked me the same question, I would probably say no, which would be either a one or a two, depending on how cold it had been and what I had been doing." Now it is my turn to smile.

"Oh." She is unsure of what to say; something has come into her life from outside the pages of fashion magazines and sales seminars.

"Why don't we forget the questionnaire," I offer.

She SMILES again. "Okay!" she exclaims. "By the way, mister, what do you do?"

Don't even think of it that way. Instead: "I teach at UAH."

"Really?" She reflects on that in a way I have become accustomed to seeing lately. My bet is that "college professor" as an occupational category lands somewhere between "policeman" and "weirdo." "What do you teach?"

"Organizational communication," I say, expecting and receiving the puzzle that her face turns into when I say it.

"Wow! That must be neat!" she says, her words belying her nonverbal expressions.

"I like it."

"Yeah, I bet!" she exclaims. It occurs to me that I read an article in one of those fashion magazines lately on how to talk to strangers, and the author gave the old Dale Carnegie pitch to "get the other person to talk about himself" and to "respond positively to whatever he is saying."

"Do you go to school?" I ask, as innocent as a fox.

She makes a FACE. "No, not anymore. I did once, though. To Calhoun. I took an English class and the teacher didn't like my spelling."

"Didn't *like* your spelling? You mean you don't spell well."

FACE PAUSES TO CONSIDER QUESTION.

"No, I mean the teacher didn't like my spelling. I spell okay. Nobody ever complains at my job. I mean, so what if I don't put two o's on certain toos? Or two l's someplace where there already is one, and everybody knows what it means anyway?"

I nod. I've heard similar complaints from my students. "Yes, but isn't that what you are going to school for? To learn how to do something better than you already know how to do it?"

"No way, Jose. I went to school to get a degree. That degree would mean that someday I could be in management. That's all I wanted. I mean, like I said before, who really cares about spelling?"

"I guess your English teacher did."

"That's right." BIG DEADLY SMILE. "And how much money is he making?"

This whole conversation has been done in a pleasant, matter-of-fact tone.

Inside both of us are no doubt convinced that we are right. Inside both of us are privately steaming—her at the injustice of English teachers and their arguments about spelling, me at the way in which money transcends every argument about spelling or learning—and both of us are caught, momentarily, in a memorable episode about each other's day that will be repeated, reenacted, with each of us emerging victorious, right, and true.

Each of us has lost the argument on grounds that the other wouldn't agree to, which is to say that each of us wins the argument on the same, but different grounds. Our communication directed toward the other is really meant for ourselves, our ritual is irrevocably interrupted, and if we are to continue at all, it must be on some other subject about which we can, possibly, reach agreement.

However, arguments between humans in the last quarter of the twentieth century do not always correspond to ancient theories of argumentation. Once our values have been questioned by other values, once our sense of self has been tagged by the other team, we simply stop doing business.

Why aid and abet the enemy?

Why put your money where your mouth isn't?

Out of the material of that simple but suggestive conversation, the phrase that haunts my mind is "That degree would mean that someday I could be in management." Zero in on the verb following the authority of that personal pronoun "I," the state-of-being verb "could be." *I could be in management.*

"In management" is a common source of fashionable cultural aspiration, another place Plato lives in *The Republic* of everyday American organizational life, a place Earl Shorris has taught us to fear not for the evil of what "management" people do, but instead for the tyranny that "management" people inspire, which is the singular power to define what ought to make us happy, which is, increasingly, to "be in management." For most people this is an unattainable dream, which helps explain why many people will tell you they are unhappy with their jobs. It isn't necessarily the work they do, but the state of being they achieve at work, that makes the difference.

Even for those "fortunate" enough in their search for the state of being that is called "being in management," happiness is seldom, if ever, achieved. This is because once that ideal form of human "being" is attained, there always exists another higher plane of happiness, higher up in this or that organization, that, theoretically, can be attained. As Shorris has it, the result is that we can never be happy so long as we allow others to define our happiness for us.

Maybe our cosmetics clerk has a valid point. I mean, from the Parisian's point of view it may not matter if happiness should be spelled with one l or two, so long as the state of being in management is.

I walk away from the counter wearing a grim smile.

I secretly enact, in the privacy of my own imagination, that one critical scene in which she loses her chance at a more perfect state of being because of poor spelling, and chuckle out loud. But then in the next breath I catch the true implication of this little narrative lie, which is that I am, after all, only trying to make myself, my argument, my values, into something superior, which is undoubtedly only one ugly way to tap into a renewable source of self-pity.

This is why I am not always the hero.

The Organizational Climate at Intimate Apparel

The next counter to catch my eye is armed by a fetching, full-figured brunette.

Only after my eyes are caught in the web of her full-figured brunettism do I recognize that she is selling lingerie. At Parisian's, however, she is not really selling "lingerie" because, at Parisian's, "lingerie" doesn't really exist. At Parisian's, in keeping with the Parisian's Point of View, where there was once lingerie there is now only "intimate apparel."

How "intimate apparel" came to replace "lingerie" (which is decidedly more French and therefore more in keeping with the name of the store) is not a question I have the clothing to ask. Is the apparel "intimate" because it lies next to private parts? Or because it is seen only by those who have the intention to become intimate? Or because, if you are wearing such clothing, you will somehow signal to those with whom you want to become intimate that something's going on?

Maybe the purchase of intimate apparel, instead of just lingerie, is the purchase of the words about the products, and all that those words can, and do, suggest? After all, if you had to choose between "intimate" and "lingerie," which one would you really choose?

Today, Ms. Full-Figured Brunette is surrounded by lacy pink underthings, and when I approach her she is fiddling with the lay of the lace on a white mannequin's nighty. I am struck by the fact that her lips match the color of the underwear surrounding her and that, as the person behind the intimate apparel counter, she is attired in many layers of clothing. Her name, at least her name as she claims it on her nametag, is CATHERINE.

"How may I help you?" she sings in the same suggestive tones as the singers advertising the Parisian point of view. The more formal "may" replaces the easier "can" in the "help you" move from cosmetics to intimate apparel. Serious business here, particularly, I have learned, when the sex of the customer is male.

"Just looking," I sing back. It occurs to me that may not be an appropriate response here, but what the hell.

"Fine. If you need any help, just let me know. My name is CATHER-INE." She says all of these words by rote, placing emphasis, as if reciting a tiresome poem, on every last word in every relevant phrase: *help, know, CATHERINE.* I also notice that she doesn't have the fun in her voice that cosmetics (what was her name? Cindy? Not CYNTHIA?) seemed to display. Maybe intimate apparel is socially embarrassing to her, or maybe she has designed her performance this way to ward off the untoward comments of customers.

I look around. What strikes me about this counter is its lack of playfulness. Lingerie, excuse me—intimate apparel—is basically trimmed-up underwear and therefore should, to my mind, represent a playful side of our consumer culture. Consider, for example, the various catalogue outlets for these fantasies, which obviously address in a very straightforward manner exactly what these symbols are suggesting.

Here, however, there is none of that.

The counter displays a variety of soft and silky stuff, from reds to pinks to fleshtones, with an equal variety of lacy designs and patterns, but that's about it. It is as if it is saying, "Look here: These are *respectable* garments for *respectable* ladies, despite their [the garments, if not the ladies'] origins." Nothing kinky, nothing edible, nothing with special doors or windows or embroidered slogans.

Today there are two ladies by the counter looking over the goods. One of them must be in her sixties, and she is obviously enjoying herself. She leans over to me and with coffee-stained breath explains that she is buying these for her daughter.

"I see," I say. But I don't.

"She's a good little girl," the woman continues, "maybe a little *too* good, if you know what I mean . . ."

I clear my throat.

"Her husband ran off and left her with two kids, but I know she has a boyfriend." A GREASY LITTLE GIGGLE ABOUT HERE.

I have always been the kind of guy older women talk to in stores. It's hard to explain. I mean there I am at the intimate apparel counter (or alone with the lettuce at the supermarket, or standing in line at the license bureau) minding my own business and an old blue-hair will inevitably sidle up to me with a question or comment. Being a basically friendly type, I will then engage in a dialogue aimed at getting at the truth about colors of underwear, varieties of lettuce, license fees, and so on.

"Do you like the bright red ones or these little pinkies?" She dangles two pairs of immodest, lace-trimmed short-shorts before my eyes.

"I don't know," I say, tentatively. "The red ones are more assertive, but the pink ones suggest a bit more subtlety." Here I am reminded of Basil Bernstein's classic work on class-specific language codes. He identified a major problem of the middle class as the ability to see too many options, an ability, he suggests, that tends to make us less able to arrive at decisions.

"I like the red ones, always did," the lady responds. Bernstein also found that members of the lower classes and upper classes use fewer words to construct thoughts and that those words tend to dichotomize the world into good/bad, right/wrong, or in this case, red/pink categories, thus making decision making easier, if less able to take into account the options and alternatives represented by a more expanded middle-class vocabulary. "The redder and skimpier, the better," she continues.

"Why not buy both? That way you can't go wrong."

"No, I'm going to stick with the red. Red stands out, you know. And that's what this girl needs!"

I redden. I guess I stand out, too, because CATHERINE comes over.

CATHERINE moves in front of us, hands clasped gently in front of her ———, "do no evil" spot.

The blue-hair hands over the red pair. "Wrap 'em up, honey," she says.

CATHERINE accepts them and asks whether this will be cash or charge.

"Oh, cash," replies the blue hair. Then she turns to me. "Why don't you go ahead and buy those little pink ones you like so much?"

"Oh, no thanks," I manage. "My wife doesn't go in for that sort of thing." Everybody seems to relax on the word "wife," including me.

CATHERINE rings up the sale, then carefully places the intimate apparel in a Parisian's floral-print bag. She returns to the blue-hair, hands her the bag. "Thank you for shopping at Parisian's," she says, but her smile lacks enthusiasm.

While this has been going on, the other consumer at the intimate apparel counter, a woman more nearly my own age, well-dressed, wearing what I believe is Obsession, has been gathering up a slinky silk night gown.

CATHERINE moves toward her and the moment of actual sale naturally approaches.

"Do you have this in an eight?" the woman asks. Her voice is strikingly superior for no reason I know of except the tendency I have observed in women about this age to engage in definite superior/subordinate communication practices, with each woman refusing in her own way to play the subordinate.

"An eight?" CATHERINE says quizzically, as if doubting that an eight would fit the purchaser's body. "Are you sure?"

"Are these sized small or something?"

A moment passes. "Well, not really. But I wear an eight." SMILE. UPRAISED EYEBROWS. HAND MOTION.

"Do you? I would have thought maybe a twelve."

"Oh no. I'm a natural eight." CATHERINE retorts.

"Amazing. If you have this in an eight I'll take it."

CATHERINE REACHES DOWN BELOW THE COUNTER AND RISES WITH AN eight. "Will this be all for today?" she recites.

"No. I want these [pantyhose]. And that, too." The customer points to a red underfit in the display case.

"What size?"

Icy silence.

CATHERINE explains. "These are sized small, medium, and large."

"Medium," replies the customer, icily.

"Will this be cash or charge?" CATHERINE DOES NOT LOOK AT THE CUSTOMER.

"Charge." The customer, after fumbling through at least six or seven charge cards searching for the right one, finally hands CATHERINE an American Express Gold Card.

"Do you have a Parisian's charge?" CATHERINE begins ringing up the sale.

"No, I don't."

"I can give you an application. There is a no-interest feature, you know."

"Yes, I know. But no thank you. I don't like acquiring credit cards."

CATHERINE completes the transaction in silence, hands the customer her floral-print bag containing the goods, and smiles squarely but does not say "thank you."

"*Bitch,*" she mouths under her breath.

This episode won't make for much of a story for either CATHERINE or the customer despite its obvious underlying dramatic tension and delicate conversational interplay. Probably the customer will derive little satisfaction from the sale, or will only wear the goods on days when she feels quietly left out of things. On those days they will feel like she is wearing nothing special.

LEAVING PARISIAN'S

On the way out of the store I pass by brand names I am supposed to respect: Member's Only, Jantzen, Nike, Reebok, Calvin Klein, Calvin Klein, Calvin Klein.

In these small, brand-name havens, sales clerks mingle with the clientele, guides selling the principles of their products as well as their seasonal appeal. I am on my way out now, and do not stop.

From the end of the store that opens out into the continuous, high-pitched hum of the mall, I look back inside and see the choreographed dance of sales activity. I also see men beginning work on the centerpiece section, taking down the televisions, carrying ladders up the stairs. I ask the white-lab-coated clerk by the Clinique counter what is happening.

"Who knows?" she says. "Management can't decide what to do with it."

"No more candy?"

"No more candy."

"That's too bad," I say, almost automatically. "That's the one part of the store I really liked."

"Yeah, a lot of men say that." She sighs. "But men don't buy anything up there. They just want to walk around and look at everything."

"Why do you suppose they do that?"

She shrugs. "I dunno. Down here in women's fashion and cosmetics most men feel stupid. They go upstairs and see candy and think, 'Here's something I know all about.' But the candy we sell up there is all imported stuff—nothing that says Hershey's—so after a while they learn not to go up there."

"Is that why you don't see many men in here?"

"Maybe." She thrusts her hands into the pockets of her lab coat. "Men need to be feel smart, in control of the situation. But when you give them that, they think they have everything."

"So they don't buy much?"

"That's right. In so many ways this store is just high school, all over again." She turns and eventually walks over to a waiting customer.

I didn't notice her name.

Out in the mall area I sit down by the fountain with older men in mostly white shirts and polyester pants, men from the previous generation of smokers.

Nobody talks; the noise of the falling water is enough. Gray smoke curls up against silvery water curling down. A woman spanks her child, who turns red and screams a bit before giving up.

"You're not old enough to go in a store by yourself, Robert," she says. "You know that."

Robert doesn't say anything.

RECESSIONAL

Back out on University Drive there is an accident.

A man, apparently a young man, tried to turn into the mall on the end of a yellow light and was destroyed by a delivery truck with the same essential attitude. Everyone is in a hurry, cars move around the wreckage and scatter the bloodied chrome and glass. In the distance an ambulance announces itself, but it can't seem to move through the traffic and it is too late anyway.

I am stuck in the other lane, watching. A man with a thick, unkempt beard parks his cart by the Do Not signs and renders assistance. Expertly, he begins to direct the traffic.

Overhead an airliner turns for its final approach.

I am speechless.

6

How I Spent My Summer Vacation

Of course we are all supposed to belong to the Castle, and there's
supposed to be no gulf between us, and nothing to be bridged over,
and that may be true enough on ordinary occasions, but we've had
grim evidence that it's not true when anything really important
crops up.

—Franz Kafka, *The Castle*

I arrived in Salt Lake City alone and apprehensive for the conference.

My apprehension was induced by the fact that it was the first time I
would be presenting a paper to this particularly esteemed group of
unknown colleagues, colleagues whose work had guided me but colleagues nonetheless whose names I was unable to associate with faces,
faces being particularly important to me at this time when everyone I
knew was old enough now to have earned one.

This faceless, situationally induced fear was framed by that intemperate
zone of the cerebral that calls itself "the emotions" but actually lives, as
Clifford Geertz puts it, as "half ungestured feeling and half unfelt ges-
ture," a place where imagined scenes from professional and personal
demise are acted out *sans merci,* a rehearsal stage for the exotic, unnameable
indignities I felt I would eventually suffer because of what I would say.

True enough, it was only a paper, a conference paper vaguely solicited,
about twenty pages of double-spaced word processing, that held the
meanings I hoped to convey. However, this single paper represented
more than a year's scholarly work (which, as any scholar knows, is
cognitively a far longer chronicle of starts and errors, moments of extreme
clarity followed by moments of absolute despair because that clarity is
discovered to be no more than what it is—the cull of the merely common-
place overstuffed with self-absorption), a year in a life that was adding
up, on the career side, to be less satisfying than everyone I valued felt it
ought to have been by now, a year marked by the granting of tenure for
work that I was no longer proud of. I had never felt this slow before.

This paper was, for me, the only way out of this emotional malaise.
It was an experiment in interpretive ethnography, a piecing together of
autobiography and observation in the form of a short story, a narrative

118

that broke all the rules. The reason why it was so important to me, particularly at this time in my career, was a little too clear. My father had told me there were only two big mistakes a man could make in his life—to choose either the wrong career or the wrong woman. I was afraid I had chosen the wrong career.

For six years I had been a junior faculty member at an aspiring but relatively unknown institution. Every day of those six years I had spent learning the trade, particularly those parts of the trade that deal with reading and writing, making "scholarly contributions" to the literature of the field. But increasingly I felt estranged. I no longer believed in what I was contributing; instead, I believed that a big part of the life of organizations was absent from our literature, and that in continuing to ignore it I was only deepening the ignorance.

I felt I had lost enthusiasm for my subject. I knew I had lost enthusiasm for reading the learned term papers that seemed to be what my discipline believed in. I feared the worst.

There seemed to me to be only two choices. Either I could leave the profession and pursue some other trade, or I could try to show other members of my profession a better alternative. Either choice was risky, but either one was preferable to continuing on this way, collecting paychecks for the next thirty years or so for expressing sentiments I no longer believed in.

I decided to devote one year—my tenure-earning year—to one essay that would, for me, determine my professional fate. If it failed, as I was almost certain it would fail, then the fraud I always feared I would end up being would come to a quick but complete fruition. I would have to quit my job, return to some ruined, solitary place in the strip-mined regions of West Virginia where nobody ever knew me and whence anyone with any sense of true dignity had long sense fled, and live there forever in a trailer with only a bed, a bottle, and an AM radio.

Such were the true dimensions of my apprehension, the extreme territories of the unknown within that carried about as much weight as a shadow does in daylight, weight being the ordinary measure of burden, but this apprehension being so complete as to fail to be measured by anything so ordinary, being so ethereal a thing itself as to escape weight entirely.

In his letter to me the director of the conference wrote that if I stood on the Salt Lake City sector of the large world map that was the center floor of the Salt Lake City airport at precisely 6:00 P.M., a graduate student would arrive to drive me to the conference.

I could be recognized not by who I was, but only by where I was standing. This fact made me oddly uncomfortable, and, given my otherwise afflicted state, proved to be the edge beyond which I could not trespass.

I planned my arrival for 10:30 that morning and forked over forty bucks to hire a cab to carry me to Alta. The first thing I remember about the trip was its lack of humidity, a fact of great importance if one comes, as I did, from Alabama in August, a state made up more and more of refugees from cold winters who learn to live half the year pent-up in refrigerated spaces in this promised land made inhabitable for them only with the advent of air conditioning. The second thing I remember was the driver's insistence that his air conditioner worked, a fact I had never doubted and a doubt I had never expressed, and his apparent need to demonstrate the empirical reality against my small complaints to the contrary.

College professors are known to be a strange lot, presented to the public on television as either boobs-with-a-brain or brains-with-no-boobs, depending on the gender. Given this media surround, the still proud among us have learned to exploit our assumed oddity for the singular purpose of getting our own way. As the air conditioner went on, my window went down; when the driver said, "This is a *strong* air conditioner," I responded, "What *high* mountains you have." He switched off the mobile refrigeration unit after I answered his question about what I did for a living, and went on to say that he had never liked school much anyway.

The conference was being held at a lodge just above Snowbird, up in the thinner air that lives at eight thousand feet above sea level, which was about seven thousand, four hundred and twenty feet higher than I was used to.

Everyone up there is healthy and sun-tanned. No one smokes, thrives on caffeine, or is impolite. Everywhere is beautiful. There are no shops or stores, no advertisements for car dealerships, and no noises of any kind.

All is air and space and mountains and wonder.

There are no televisions in the rooms, nor is there a radio anywhere in the lodge. You come here in winter to ski, in summers to hike, and on

Sundays to enjoy one of the world's most impressive buffets. I came a day ahead of a conference with strangers, without the proper shoes and without film for my camera, further evidence of what anticipation can do to a thirty-three-year-old man for whom the movement of days and trains are increasingly seen as essentially the same.

I walked into the lodge, which meant out of the close and vivid sun and into a cool and calm environment where I was immediately greeted by a handsome young woman at the front desk who called me by my nickname.

I had never seen her before.

I had never been here before. Was this the front desk receptionist in a perfect American heaven?

As it turned out, my secretary had made my reservations here using the nickname and the receptionist was just being friendly. She asked me to drop my bags and accompany her back down the corridor I had just entered, back through the door that had brought me inside. She then commanded me to walk down about a hundred yards to a silvery rock on the other side of the road, turn around, and walk back.

When you are a stranger in a strange land you do what the natives tell you to do. I walked down to the rock, turned around, and got about halfway back before I found that the air in my lungs could no longer sustain my life. I stopped. I gasped. I slowly regained consciousness that was accompanied by a new heaviness in my legs and lightness in my head. The receptionist took my arm and led me slowly back inside the lodge. "The point of this exercise," she said, "was to show you the importance of knowing where you are and what being here can do to you."

I like to drink. Not heavily, but regularly.

I had been warned by the friendly receptionist that two drinks at this altitude feel like four stiff ones anywhere else. But in the gentle moments of that first evening, as I watched the western light fade into the valley and a mute symphony of twinkling stars collect around me, life seemed perfect and light and true. So I finished two ordinary drinks.

The first one went down quickly, smoothly. During its life I relived part of my own, the part that took from undergraduate to graduate school, then to a three-year teaching stint, a year of regular work in an organization, and then back to graduate school to complete my formal education. These were fun years, full of promise and challenge. I was searching for some honorable something to commit to, a purpose higher than an occupation, a way of life that would add up to a full life.

So much of it was accident that the rest of it seemed like chance. But perhaps not. As an only child growing up in a diplomat's household that changed it premises every two and one-half years, moved its language, relationships, and culture to another language, new relationships, and culture, perhaps it was inevitable that communication, relationships, and culture would become the natural objects of my curiosity. We tend to study that which we feel we don't do very well.

It is also true that my father led a dual life and was a broken poet, a fact I did not know until after he died and his diaries became my possession. I remember growing up with visits from literary figures, still have a small book of poems given to him in Rome by Ezra Pound, inscribed "To Lloyd, a good kid and great life poet damned by this Christ-forsaken world." He never published a line, but encouraged me to.

The second drink came. I don't remember ordering it. During its life I passed naturally into the current phase of mine. Summed up it came to this: Mostly I didn't want to disappoint my wife. She had married me on the promise that I would pursue my writing. I had done that, but with textbooks and articles form the *Quarterly Journal of Speech,* etc., that through my own failures to be honest with my work had not amounted to much.

It was my own fault. But it could still be turned around. Right here.

I walked back to my room feeling fine.

The next morning it felt like I had finished two bottles. The sun was a brutal yellow reminder of my last resolve never to drink again and to become a better Christian person. A headache in the Rockies, as I learned the hard way, moves beyond mere pain into a paralyzing pounding of merciless agony, the kind of thing you would only in your worst moment wish on someone who had utterly destroyed all that was meaningful and happy in your life.

I was in PAIN.

I figured I had about four hours to make it from the bed to the aspirin I hoped I had remembered to pack in the bag that was now laughing at me from the bathroom. Four hours hence the conference would start; if I could not remedy this headache in four hours I was sure my life as I had known it would begin to end.

Aspirin, like the inner workings of a microchip, is for me pure magic.

I might as well admit it. It either does the job or it doesn't, and either way there is no way for a mere mortal like me to explain it. In the case of a microchip, when it fails to work I call a technician who casts electronic spells on the machine until the digital magic works again. In the case of aspirin, when it fails I call upon God.

I began my prayer by stating that I was indeed a sinner, unworthy of His trust or comfort in this, my time of need, but hoping for one last outside chance to prove myself if only He would intervene directly and remove the aching parts of my brain, replacing them with the calm that I was by that time certain only He could provide. It came out somewhat less eloquently, sounding something like this: "Uuuuuuuuuuuuhhhhhh-hhhhhhhhhhhhhh."

I ended up being totally and shamelessly repentant.

Sometimes it works. And this time it did.

It was then that I discovered that I was indeed too tall a person to rent a room here.

This discovery was made when I opened the shower curtain to see that the shower nozzle was aimed squarely at my navel. God had relieved my headache but was still nursing a grudge against me.

I went down on my knees in that porcelain place and washed myself with a new brand of scented soap provided by the lodge and an old brand of shampoo I had brought with me. The combination of scents made me into a sort of fragrant, herbal presence that, if you would have passed in a tight place, would have at least given you cause for an illiberal form of wonder. Thus emasculated, and still suffering from panic reconstruction in the head, I put on a smart summer suit and walked out into a room full of strangers dressed down in jeans and T-shirts.

They immediately assumed I was from the South.

I learned this later when the conference director said that one of the reasons he had invited me was that while he and his colleagues had admired my work, they collectively felt that if I had stayed in Huntsville, Alabama, this long there was probably a good reason for it, a suspicion confirmed when I entered the room wearing what, in this culture of academics, were clearly the wrong clothes.

This is the age in America when everyone who is anyone speaks, as Allison Lurie puts it, "the language of clothes." Ours has become a stylish and expanding vocabulary of adornment opportunities, opportunities that make claims about not only who you are, but moreover who you want to be treated as being in that "other" life you only pretend in—cowboy Ralph Laurens, young Madonnas, macho bomber pilots, calculated horn-rimmed, pencil-pocketed nerds. Our individual searches for excellence these days must come dressed for success. I knew this but failed anyway.

There I was, a man in a light-blue suit with an Alexander Julian tie, surrounded by joggers and mountain climbers and other varieties of the physically aware. My nonverbal mistake was obvious, so I did what I could to try to fit in. I loosened my tie, removed my jacket, and said, "Howdy." Here I was, a man who smelled like a flower garden, looked like a stockbroker, talked like a Texan, and wore no suntan despite hailing from the land of sunshine.

I figured that if things got any worse I could always go home. I still had a wife and two dogs who would recognize and love me. After all, even a man who fails at first appearances and who is about to make a public fool out of his professional self must preserve some sense of pride.

It was then, I think, that the conference director took me aside. He asked me if I would mind postponing my paper until tomorrow, due to a scheduling problem. I said "yes" before thinking, which when I thought about it really meant "no, I don't mind," which I then said a little louder than I meant to. He squinted at me and smiled. "Good," he said.

This change in plans gave me a convenient excuse to return to my room and change clothes on the pretense of merely depositing the twenty-odd copies of my paper I had carried with me. Once back there I rummaged through my luggage to find the one pair of jeans I had brought along. As I removed my tie and kicked off my dress shoes I thought about it and changed my mind.

What the hell, they had already seen me dressed as the fool they assumed I was, no point in proving it now by changing clothes just to fit in.

I could leave my jacket and tie behind, but not my self-respect.

The conference opened with a short introduction by the director.

He apologized for the changes in scheduling, due to last-minute cancellations by a couple of the grander scholars I had hoped to impress. He gave their excuses and they all seemed real: one was pregnant and didn't want to fly, another was consulting and needed the money, a third was off to work in a refugee camp, a cause we all knew he was committed to.

The director suggested we go around the room and introduce ourselves and our affiliations. We did. Everyone seemed friendly, happy to be there. I flashed back to the last convention I had attended where the opposite seemed the case, where we wore the obligatory name tags that marked us as noteworthy or not in places like elevators and bars, and your whole being was summed up by some vague association between your last name and your last contribution to the literature. And, of course, the little animal emblems that explain where you went to school.

After the first day I removed my nametag. I never owned an animal emblem.

The first presentation was by Professor H.

I knew this one was going to be an intense intellectual exercise when he began by saying that he was interested in differentiating "the here and now from the there and then." He then proceeded to make this strange set of words into a symbolic turning point in the whole history of postmodern psychology, with particularly insightful references to the human relations movement and its effects on organizational theories of interpersonal communication and motivation. At one point he argued that two well-known syndromes previously associated with advanced alcoholism were, in fact, synonymous with sound organizational communication principles.

The first syndrome, in which a patient continuously forgets what he or she has just said in order to adjust to the booming, buzzing demands of the ever-present now, corresponds to the adaptive theory of management, in which previous decisions, discussions, and meanings are readily abandoned in favor of whatever it takes to stay in control of the present. The second syndrome, in which a patient mimics exactly the words spoken to her or him in a constant and extreme attempt to always fit in, mimics also the posturing the research literature had associated with positive feedback and cultural stability.

What makes these correspondences possible? How is it that signs of alcoholic madness and theories of organizational communication could be integrally related? It is, he said, the language of a postmodern, capitalistic world, a time and place and its words.

Professor H., who was attired during this performance in a pair of cut-offs, sandals, and a gray Oxford University T-shirt across which dangled a pair of designer sunglasses, continued his presentation by arguing that the problem of human relations in organizations has been compounded recently by the turn of our society from symbols of meaning to signs of signification. In the romanticized past (the "there and then"), meanings seemed fuller than they do now, a fact I had long suspected given my own preferences for old cars and 60's music, and when a gift was given, whether that gift was a hug or a diamond ring, its meaning was associated with symbolic closeness between people.

However, in the postmodern rush toward consumerism, gifts are now associated with signs of status, signs of getting ahead or of doing well. This explains why we sometimes feel jilted when the present we get on Christmas morning doesn't equal the one we gave. It also explains a way of understanding how meaning has been replaced (in the here and now) with signification, another cause of our incessant need to romanticize the past. Furthermore, this theory can be used to explain why it is that we seem to be encouraged, in organizational life, to "consume ourselves," our sense of who and what we are worth being dependent on signs of status that are increasingly meaningless or at best less fulfilling after we have them than we think they ought to be before they become ours. "Is this all there is?" becomes an excuse to go out and buy yet another object in an attempt to get one true moment of feeling out of an otherwise insignificant, bureaucratic life.

So on we go, from high to high, not a habit of drugs chemical, but of a drug made out of signs, in a society we increasingly can't understand because the past (the "there and then") feels better than the present (the "here and now") and the future is only a larger debt already incurred by our need to consume mistaken for our real need, which is to *mean*.

While I was listening to this talk I was thinking about myself and my own need to consume. As a collector of old cars I could see my victimage in a language I had never known before. I had, it was true, gone through about thirty cars in the past five years, each one giving me an unnatural high for an increasingly littler while, my desire for possession now darkly unmasked as a truer desire for consumption, an obsession rooted, as I now understood it, in the emptiness that was my professional, organizational life. And now, at this conference, a scholar dressed as a jogger had confirmed this to be exactly the case.

It was more than my clothing that now worried me.

It was my paper, the symbol that meant, at least to me, my way out of professional meaninglessness, the easy completion of articles and books that were only done as signs, as extra paychecks with which to buy more cars, as signals of my own way of consuming my self, the professional self that I had always hoped was somewhere within me. If I failed now, then what?

A bed, a bottle, and an AM radio alone in a trailer park, one lost cause insisting merely on existing in West Virginia, done in at last by symbols of my own making. I would have then consumed myself, become "rotten with perfection" in my own promised land.

What troubled me now was the way my paper was written. This had been my choice, my purpose, but now I questioned that decision in light of the fact that I would be the one actually reading it. In this room, to this audience. Soon.

Had I simply wanted to be different? To stand out in the crowd? I knew this wasn't the case but no one else did.

Maybe I was just setting myself up so I could take the big fall. I became uncomfortable with myself.

The next presentation was by Professor B.

He looked about right to me, which means only that he more or less resembled what I had previously assumed. He is a large man who wears jeans and a regular shirt comfortably, a man who lives in Texas comfortably, a man who is also comfortable with words.

He handed out a copy of his work-in-progress to each of us, and each of us made an attempt to decipher it until he began. He began by saying that he wanted to argue that the decision to launch the space shuttle *Challenger* was the right decision, given contemporary theories of innovative management, and that the resulting explosion of it in the air above Cape Canaveral that caused the death of its astronauts was not a "normal accident."

A "normal accident"—a term borrowed from the book by the same title by Charles Perreau—is not an accident merely reported on the evening news or written about in the newspapers after the fact. It is an accident with heavier symbolic import, in this case an accident we all witnessed *in vivo* on our television screens, an accident that included not just former test pilots but a female schoolteacher, and an accident whose forewarnings had not been completely taken into account when the decision to launch was made. The point was, he went on to say, that when discourse about a non-normal accident gets going, it becomes entropic, increasing with its randomness its velocity of decay, and the result is a form of national panic pervaded by a guilty sense of helplessness.

He paused. In the space of that pause I reflected upon what he had just said. I lived in Huntsville, the home of NASA's Marshall Space Flight Center, the home also of three schools named for the three dead Apollo astronauts killed when their rocket exploded on the launch pad, a town alive with the spirit of the stars and recently filled with this guilty sense of helplessness over the *Challenger* accident. It was Marshall that was called on the carpet for the decision to launch; it was my university that had only a few months before awarded an honorary doctorate to Judy Resnick, the other female killed in the accident; and it was I who had applied to become the first teacher in space and had secured my national professional association's nomination.

When that rocket exploded, my city, my university, and I were the lowest places on the blue planet. Professor B.'s thesis was in part a vindication, because his work on Marshall's decision making gave them a clean bill of health (given the current state of management and decision-making theory) and because he believed that tragic as that accident was, it had been in fact blown way out of proportion. Do you know how many test pilots are killed every year? Does the nation stop to honor them? Is the efficiency of the decision-making machinery in the combined Departments of Defense called into question when each one dies? Is the goal of their effort criticized?

Now partially vindicated, I was also partially aggravated. Had I too become a victim of a high-tech rhetoric that promised safe space travel? Had that part of me that identified closely with the astronauts been unnecessarily slain by weapons no more or less powerful than the spoken words of public relations personnel? And because I was a student of organizational communication, and especially of rhetorical theories, had I been so easily, so completely, duped?

B. went on. He laid out his argument for all to see, complete with a chart of the decision-making hierarchy at Marshall, a black circle drawn around the name of the man who made the decision not to tell his superior about a few engineers' worries about the effects of cold weather on the O-ring seal.

Here my heart sank. I knew a few of those engineers who worked at NASA, at Thiokol, at Rockwell, and at Sperry. I knew them because they had shown up more than a bit chagrined in continuing education classes I had offered on presentational speaking skills. They all told about the same story, a story that begins with an undergraduate degree from a school of engineering that does not require a course in speech, a story that continues with their professor's insistence that numbers and facts "speak for themselves," and so what is the need for a course that would merely delay their graduation—a story that ends about five to seven years down the career path they have collectively walked, a path that leads them into a management life of talking, arguing, negotiating, and presenting for which they are ill equipped. This is when they go back to classes like mine to learn what they should have learned years before and should have been encouraged to practice every day since.

Some of them over the years had expressed concerns to me about the shuttle program. These concerns were expressed in unlikely, uncreditable places—around coke machines at break time, mostly. I had heard them, expressed my well-intentioned sorrow for their plight, and shuffled with them back to class. Maybe if I had been a better teacher, they would have been better advocates for their concerns. Maybe if I had listened more carefully to their words, I would have learned about the O-ring seal problem before it caused a national disaster, maybe I could have used my own abilities to argue for them.

This was, of course, a situationally induced fantasy. Like most fantasies, and particularly those professional ones that come to you at conventions, it was part truth and a whole lot fancy. The truth was contained in my objections to the education provided to engineers and to my belief that a better skilled speaker could have made the point more vividly, with more rhetorical force. And there was truth in the fact that engineers in my classes had expressed concerns about the shuttle all along. All the rest was fancy nonsense, featuring fearless me as the all-time hero, the man who could have changed the world.

As a lone star lost in this heady, fantastic space I didn't catch the rest of Professor B.'s presentation about the shuttle. I nodded at the end of it, though, made the appropriate grunting noises academics typically associate with reflective stimulation. I regret this because Professor B.'s work was genuinely stimulating, and his thesis, though incomplete by his own standards, was worthy of serious consideration.

That night we dined together on fresh salmon.

The air was cool and clear, the conversation, in the early going, was work. As it turned out, Professor C. had horses, so we spoke of horses for a while. And there was a native Californian in our midst, so we talked

California, a conversation joined by Professor R. and one of her graduate students, a big friendly guy who I later learned was reared in Nebraska, both of whom thought there was no better place than L.A. to live or to consult in.

The salmon was perfect, and I ate it, despite the fact that I had claimed for years to be allergic to it. This was a claim made on the basis of a choice I made the day after one particularly memorable long night when food (in this case salmon) mixed with drink (in this case cheap wine and dry martinis), produced an enormous sickness the next morning. I invented the allergy to salmon rather than to alcohol to save face with my wife who didn't drink much and who also didn't think I should. After that statement I was repulsed by the thought of salmon, and on at least one occasion I nearly became legitimately ill on account of that thought.

But I ate this salmon anyway, just to fit in.

I didn't drink, just in case.

The next morning I felt fine but took two aspirin anyway. I did this as a hedge against the headache I expected to arrive at the moment I began reading my paper, a headache being the cerebral forewarning of impending doom.

I pulled on my blue jeans and looked in the mirror. Is this the man I had become? Thirty-three years old, hair still blond but thinning and receding as if in steady retreat from all that I saw, midsection threatening to lop over my belt, the handles on my sides making me look there like a fleshy vase making a clear statement about gluttony. Aristotle said that a man's body was best between the ages of thirty and thirty-five, and the mind reached its zenith at forty-nine. If this is what my body looked like at thirty-three, maybe it was a sign that I was in trouble on the road to forty-nine.

On the other hand, Scott Fitzgerald said that a man reached his peak, mentally and physically, at twenty-seven, and he said this when he was thirty-five. It occurred to me that only the Buddhists still believe that old age, bald heads, and fat bellies are best. And here I was, just your average more-or-less Christian, a creature made only to be saved from himself by either divine intervention or an act of pure will.

I resolved to stop writing textbooks. Writing textbooks, I was sure at that moment, had made me fat. I also resolved to follow my wife's good advice about exercise. And I resolved to hold to these resolutions longer than I had before. All of these things seemed entirely possible at eight thousand feet. It is truly unfortunate that I cannot seem to sustain those truths at lower altitudes.

But on that morning anything was possible. And my shirt was light, bright, baby blue.

I began by stating that what my colleagues were about to hear was a writing experiment.

I then apologized for needing to read it to them, opposed as I usually am to outloud, verbatim renditions of one's prose. I justified my need to read on the slim promise that the words were their own message about the organization I had studied.

That sentence made me feel strangely Californian.

I nervously took in one long deep breath, and on its exhale, began.

About halfway through my presentation H. looked at D. and B. looked at H. I continued to read as they rose together and left waving quick, awkward goodbyes.

I figured they didn't like it.

I spoke a little louder.

When I finished reading I looked up at the polite but clearly puzzled faces of my colleagues.

Professor T. thanked me for sharing my story with them and went on to say that he was glad to see some interpretive work—as opposed to more interpretive theory—being done again.

There was a round of mumbles that sounded like assent.

The director added a few encouraging words after which we took a break.

During the break a couple of people told me how much they enjoyed my paper. They were sincere!

I was not a failure!

These responses were better than I had hoped for, more than I had ever gotten after reading something at a convention. I had learned not to be too disappointed. As my mentor, Professor P., had once told me, "One of the terrible truths of scholarship is that no one really cares very much what you think unless they can use it to advance their own careers." He added, kindly, "And most of what we use to advance our own careers, in the long run, doesn't really add up to very much."

He was right. In my experience the only thing shorter than the life of an academic's conference paper is the life of someone else's conference paper.

I drifted through the rest of the conference, occasionally joining in on a discussion to make some passionate point that upon reflection would have probably been better left unsaid or at least said less passionately.

The presentations were both better and worse than mine. This, of course, according to the authority of me rather than them.

But no one avoided me in the halls.

Suddenly it was over.

The conference director made a short speech in which he thanked us for our contributions, encouraged us to continue to our interpretive work.

We checked out before noon and said our awkward goodbyes.

I rode down the mountain and had a good conversation about something I can no longer remember. At the airport, with jets everywhere in the air suggesting nothing more than jets everywhere in the air, Professor A. asked me if he could share my paper with some of his graduate students as an example of how interpretive work could be done.

It was one of the nicest things any of my colleagues had ever said to me. I said so, and embarrassed him without meaning to.

Then I was on the plane rising above the Rockies, rising above my apprehension, confident again. No longer was I tired of me. How could I be?

There was a new literature to write, and to do it right meant a lifetime of work to do.

7

Notes on Method

Much current ethnographic writing depicts culture in a contested, emergent, ambiguous fashion, particularly when attached to the studies of groups and organizations deep inside complex industrial societies. . . . This is not because the methods at our disposal are imprecise or weak, but because such ambiguity is an accurate characterization of the way things are in reality. Representations should presumably be commensurate with the obscurity and shifting nature of the cultural materials themselves.

—John Van Maanen, *Tales of the Field*

Whatever else ethnography may be . . . it is above all a rendering of the actual, a vitality phrased.

—Clifford Geertz, "Being There, Writing Here"

A CONFESSION

I did not want to write this concluding chapter.

It was composed at the insistence of my editor upon the advice of at least one of my reviewers. These individuals felt that to adequately address an academic audience I would need to bring the book to a final place like this one, where I could "tie into" the existing literatures, comment on the usefulness of the study and its subversive style of writing, and make some overall estimate of what I have learned.

Perhaps they are right.

My reluctance to give in to their insistence grieves even me. After all, I was reared in academic traditions of scholarship. I know how important it is to make an argument, document it with material drawn from the literature, and show the relevance of your own small brushstrokes against the larger canvas of inquiry. I know this, but I can't do it.

Not their way. At least not here.

Casing a Promised Land celebrates a form of resistance to that argumentative impulse. What I set out to do was to show, to reveal, to represent; what is asked of me now is to tell about, to theorize, to prove or at least to argue for. At the heart of my purpose was to demonstrate that the conventions of scholarly writing could be challenged, that news could be made that did not so much tie into the literature as untie from it. That a story could do what narrative theories, organizational theories, and rhetorical theories had not done.

To write the sort of concluding essay that is required here is to suggest—no, worse, to endorse—that it is needed. Naked storytelling is maybe all right as a sideshow, but the *real* point of this book is best dressed in traditional clothes. At least wear the old school tie!

That last paragraph was fun to write, but this book is a first step and first steps often involve compromises.

You are now reading mine.

Maybe I'm afraid they are right. Besides, I know I want to see the book published and if this is all it takes to accomplish that, well . . .

This is the part where the detective cops out. Not entirely, mind you. But enough to suggest to the reader he isn't pure. Enough to remind himself of it too.

So I give. In. At least a little bit. A compromise.

It goes like this:

WHAT I SET OUT TO DO: TYING IT IN

My concern throughout this book has been to show some of the effects of living and working in a high-technology environment located in what was once the rural South.

This has been an opportunity to investigate what symbols that emerge from a high-technology and consumer-capitalism environment do to us. My objective was to detect and to meditate on that swirl of ineffable feelings and incomplete thoughts that evoke simultaneously the real and the fantastic, the facts within the fiction, the self in images of others, beginnings that are capable of defining and leading us into endings.

I have also been concerned with the mystery of writing. I approached this subject with a sense of scholarly romance for the research and writing processes, but eventually learned that the more appropriate metaphor was that of the cultural detective. When that happened I saw clearly that to complete this project would mean turning the mystery of writing into the writing of mystery.

Within the field of ethnography in particular, and social science in general, the past decade has been one of experimentation and change with forms of scholarly expression. Our literatures represent our values, attitudes, and beliefs as much as—perhaps more than—they reveal knowledge or truth about that which we claim to be studying. In ways no more nor less mystical than the secret vodoun societies of Haiti, our words create forms of cultural belief that are capable of making the living appear dead, our "methods" topical agents as powerful as their tetrodotoxin. During the past decade or so, ethnographers, "new" journalists, and scholars in disciplines that span the arts and sciences have tried to find ways of opening up scholarly writing, breathing life into the corpus of knowledge.

The issue is not as simple as good writing, although admittedly I used to think it was. Beyond the writer's tactics lies a social and political world that is as protective of the status quo as any government agency. Beyond that world lies an even broader cultural milieu, more naive but also far more powerful, a world made up increasingly of voters who demand something of value for their tax dollars. For them, the debates over our methods of research and writing are meaningless. What they collectively want is technology, ways and means of improving the quality and efficiency of their lives. For the public, our worth is often understood only in relation to the material worth of our products.

Given the upsurge of books and articles that propose the presence of an absence in higher education, there is good reason to be concerned about what we produce. For scholars experimenting with new styles of research and writing, this concern often becomes twisted into an ugly question. Put simply, the ugly question—perhaps the ugliest question in American higher education today—is "Of what use is your research?"

ANSWERING THE UGLIEST QUESTION

The reason why the usefulness of a particular style of research and writing is an ugly question lies in the task of naming its answer.

It should be enough to simply point to the story and say, "Read it, and if it informs and moves you, then it has value." But that is not enough. Instead, ethnographers have to up the ante. In this case, my particular upping of the ante goes way up, all the way to an ancient and too often forgotten scholarly purpose. For me, if I have to answer the question, my answer is *truth and beauty*.

Truth, As I See It

Like the quotations that open this chapter, I agree that how a piece of scholarship represents the reality it claims to have captured is as important as the reality it claims to have captured.

Truth, in this case representational truth, can operate only by including in the story its particulars as well as its generalities. To tell the truth means to write the account as it lived in the world, which is very different from how it lives in sentences that divide us from the world.

Perhaps you think I am leaving out some important details. For example, can "pure" description or depiction or even representation of anything actually exist? Probably not. Then how can I say that this style of research and writing is aimed at truth?

For me truth is not a place to come to through a simple accumulation of facts or through narrow definitional debates. (This does not mean, however, that I doubt the reality of that method for those who practice it. Like my preferred version of the afterlife, I believe that whatever people think will happen to them when they die, or do research, happens to them.) For me, truth is always partial, always dependent on where you are standing when you perceive it, and tangled up in the language you use to describe it. Once you utter anything about it you alter it, and in doing so induce others to see it YOUR WAY rather than in THE WAY. Is there a THE WAY? I don't know. What I do know is that for me *truth* is a word that does not begin with a capital letter. It is an ambiguous statement about a sloppy process that ends up masquerading as an outcome because it tries very hard to look like one. Truth, like the communication of it, is a process that creates relationships.

In these sentences truth is also an "it."

A beautiful, interpretable, slithery, slippery one, admittedly, but nevertheless an "it." And most importantly in my view of things, it is an "it" that changes. It seldom stands still, and never for very long. There is a difference between the true and truth—the former being commonly misunderstood as an attribute of the latter, whereas in the world I inhabit it is quite the other way around. You can make true statements, but the truth is not as easily told. Truth comes in disguises, and often pretends not to exist. What is true always exists, even when it is disputed or disguised. After all, each generation's historians reshape the truth about everything and everyone who ever lived, breathed, made whoopee, worked, or went to war. But it is still true that certain historical acts happened.

Truth is a matter for interpretation, what is true is a matter for argument. Interpretations represent perspectives and ask questions about why, how, and what for. They do not invite judgment so much as encourage discussion. Arguments attempt to win, to be judged "right," to end the discussion. They also ask questions about why, how, and what for, but their aim is the true rather than the truth. You can argue about what is true, be perfectly correct, and never get close to the truth. You can try to find truth and, along the way, learn what it isn't.

Do I believe interpretive ethnography is any better than any other method for doing this sort of research?

Really, this is pretty fancy language for something as uncomplicated as hanging out with people, taking notes on what they do and say, noticing aspects of their environments, and writing it down the best you can. You are mindful that you aren't really telling things the way they are because you aren't God and besides, things and people as well as their meaningful orders tend to change in ways that your eyes and especially your word processor can't catch.

But is it "BETTER"???

That may be the crucial issue for some of you, but not for me. "Better" is, after all, an incredibly complicated evaluation. Better for whom? Better for what? Better, can you spare me a paradigm?

No more fooling around. I promise. The answer is: Yes, actually. I think interpretive ethnography is better. It is certainly better for me. Whether that makes any difference to you is another matter. If the evaluation of "better" is tied up to the family tree of knowledge, then I think it is "better" in the sense that suggests "less precise, more open to critical scrutiny, less likely to be judged by its adherence to a method than for its statement (mostly insights) about a culture."

For me, this form of scholarly storytelling is "better" because it deals with the rhetoric of the inherently contingent, and rhetoric always deals with the contingent, and admits that it is rhetoric and that it's also dealing with the contingent. This method also invites writers to deal with the various and changing meanings that people associate with situations and makes no claims for generalizability, replicability, or infallibility. It is a situation-specific, author-specific, fallible method. It asks more questions than it pretends to answer, and its chief product is a perspectival understanding of the truth created by and constituted in a transient rhetoric.

The only difference, then, between interpretive ethnography and any other method of social science is that its practitioners seem to be more willing to admit its limitations. And, ironic as it may seem, I believe that partly because of this willingness and partly because of its beauty it will have lasting value as a cultural artifact. Which brings me to the subject of beauty.

Beauty, From the Vantage of an Academic Beast

I have always found it ironic that the discipline of communication has yet to produce any nationally recognized literary figure. If we know so much about how to communicate a message to an audience, then how come we aren't being widely read or listened to?

The answer is one of two possibilities. Either the public is not really interested in what we are writing about, or that the way we write fails to communicate to readers. Either way, the answer is not very flattering. If we are not writing about what the public thinks is important, then we had better learn how to make them believe it is important or else our future is seriously threatened. There is a strong sense of academic Darwinism in these troubled economic times. On the other hand, if we are failing to communicate to our readers, why should we claim to be authorities on the subject of communication? An authority in this area should at least embody its virtues.

You may disagree with this premise; others have. I have heard that the readers for our scholarly discourse are being communicated to because they are us and because these are the standards for scholarly discourse we have endorsed. We are an elite audience, holders of advanced degrees and sharers in a particular and highly technical language code. This gives us license for abstraction and fun in the air. Besides, our knowledge is constituted in a specialized language. Where would we be without the Greek, French, Latin, and German borrowings? In some cases, without those words we have nothing much to say.

That was nasty. And not entirely untrue. And that is the problem. Why is it that American scholars want to use foreign terms to describe American speech and culture? Why is it that our forms of scholarly discourse are derived from European models? This question has an easy and apparent answer: our nation is a melting pot and our academic institutions derived their form from earlier European models. The harder question is why, when we have modified and in most cases changed the curriculum to become the envy of the academic world, we haven't also taken a leadership role in changing the available forms of scholarly expression?

An interesting issue, perhaps. But I am going astray of beauty.

To seek the beautiful in forms of scholarly expression is neither to abandon nor to lessen the impact of what is true or the ways in which we seek the truth. It is simply to complete the process of research by attending to its counterpart—its written representation.

Beauty and truth.

Notice I did not write beauty *or* truth. Nor did I try to suggest that I am fooling around with something less serious than the full implications of these two important words, say by making debutantes out of their spelling: *Beauti* and *Truethy*. Nor did I express the sentiment this way:

BEAUTY
Truth

I wrote it exactly like I say it when I say it to make this point: Beauty and truth should go together, be spelled properly, as equal partners in the mission to communicate. Surely truth suffers and is thought less of when poorly expressed. And beauty in the place of truth has merely cosmetic appeal. Together, and in balance, they represent the best of what representation is about, which is the depiction of realities that draws us into (rather than separates us from) the experiencing of life.

James Dickey tells his writing classes (which are also research and theory-constructing classes) to "show, don't tell." Actually, his use of the language is more like this: "Show 'em, goddamnit! Don't tell 'em about it like some *pissant!*" The same advice should be used in the training of academics. To show—by which I mean to reveal descriptively—is to give access to the experience. To tell—by which I mean to analyze—is to limit the access to the experience and favor access to ideas the experience suggests. To show is better than to tell because you give the data prior to developing the idea.

Beauty should be shown, then talked about. Somehow, to talk about it before showing it always lessens its impact and invites criticism of your standards. It is to say to your reader or listener: "Look here, I want you to listen to my analysis because it is so wonderful. Never mind the scenes that produced it. Reality is lesser stuff than theory, you know."

This is the story of beauty undone.

It is a sad story, isn't it?

The Postmodern, Apocalyptic, Deconstructive Interlude

Truth and beauty. Words and music. Dialectic and rhetoric.

Writer and reader.
Writer and
Writer
Writer.

This is where I came in and where I must exit again. At least from this discussion of truth and beauty. That's why we do it the way we do it and call it interpretive ethnography. We do it for truth and beauty. Even when it is not fashionable, there is no other reason.

The Obligatory Statement for Those Who Would Practice This Art

I have been asked if ethnography is distinct from other forms of storytelling—investigative reporting, for example.

Another call for definitional debate, I suppose. Obviously, some ethnographers think so. Others apparently do not. I prefer John Van Maanen's approach to answering this question—all forms of storytelling about organizations and cultures are tales of the fieldwork, more distinctive for the individual voices of their authors and the style of the author's observations than for the separate, comparable categories of discourse.

In that spirit I personally believe that the sort of writing that I do is part autobiography and part cultural ethnography. It is not particularly different from the writing of an investigative reporter (such as Tom Wolfe, Richard Rhodes, or Joan Didon), or for that matter that of a good novelist (such as Fitzgerald, Dinesen, Kafka, O'Conner, Chandler, Didion, Hammett, Paretsky, Percy, or Hannah).

What distinguishes it is not what makes it particularly different, but what makes it particular. For me, that is the authorial voice directed toward the experience of detection. To become an organizational detective, an investigator and writer of mysteries, requires not so much an epistemological or ontological orientation as a desire to know that can only be satisfied in the act of writing.

What this means for a person who wants to pursue this line of work is not particularly new or flashy. You need to read a lot (and to do justice to the ideals of a liberal education, read a lot in a wide variety of fields), and write every day (at least three or four hours), and get out of the office more often to engage that which you desire to know about. All this takes time and effort and a little ingenuity.

However, you can do all of these things, work very hard at them, and develop nothing more than character. Unlike most other research methods carefully executed according to tradition, there is no guarantee of publishable results. That is the big risk in this sort of writing. Just doing it, even doing it to the best of your abilities, doesn't mean that what you've done is good enough. And even when it should be good enough, sometimes there is simply an absence of luck.

It is no secret that there are a lot of failed, good writers with advanced degrees waiting tables, making fine sentences, but never getting a break. As in any other organization, your best hope for advancement (beyond essential talent and hard work) is a mentor with clout. No kidding.

Read a lot, write a lot, get out of the office often. And go to the right schools. When you get there do your serious studying with people who have been around the block a few times, even though it is sometimes more appealing to fall into step with those young sharps taking their first, tentative ones. They may end up famous and well respected, but that may also happen at the expense of your education.

Hard words, these.

While you are in school take some writing classes. If you are already out of school go back and take them. Fiction, nonfiction, biography, even technical writing will help. Think of these experiences as the logical adjuncts to your research methods courses. Think of them also as opportunities to improve the most basic academic skill—writing—and the only one that will lead your words into eventual print.

Do not expect miracles. One course, or one degree program, does not a writer make. In my case it took me twelve years of reading a lot, writing every day, and going to the right schools before I ever got anything published. Maybe I was a slow learner.

And maybe not.

The process of ethnography—particularly cultural ethnography—tends to be slow. It took eight years of living in Huntsville and its environs to make this little volume, even though the actual writing required a mere two full years. When you add it all up you had better be doing it because you feel that without it you would be a lesser person. You do it because it makes your life, not your bank account, richer.

You do it, ultimately, for beauty and truth.

One more item. This one because I was really stupid when I was young and I hope no one makes the same mistake. When you get the urge—and you will get this particular urge—to proselytize, don't attack your colleagues or their methods. Remember, everyone walks around thinking (believing) she or he is essentially right. No person I know in academe practices social science in any of its forms because they are faking it. They believe in what they do. At least grant them their dignity. The democratic spirit of diversity must be maintained; after all, it is precisely that spirit that allows this sort of writing a place at the Big Table.

This does not, of course, guarantee that you and your "methods" won't be attacked. When this happens say to the attacker something like this: "Personally, I don't find answers to the questions I want to pursue in questionnaires, or in surveys, or in discussions of critical theories, or in whatever. I don't know how to count the way a person feels looking out of an office window, or how to deconstruct the simmering hatred between coworkers that manifests itself in small acts of semiotic terrorism. Nor can I be comfortable with a method that separates me, my motives, my background, my life from the subject. You may think this is mere subjectivity or absolute solipsism, and I may think that what you write is burdened by a lack of critical appraisal of your motives for writing it, or a failure to challenge yourself to adapt your message to readers other than those who collect at the same spiritual alter.

"In the end, none of this matters. Our combative rhetoric will be little more than playful tears to the real issues that live in the world beyond this battleground. It is not likely that we will ever agree. Nor is it likely that one of us will give in.

"I do this because it makes sense to me, which is, I'm sure, also why you do it differently. As Kurt Vonnegut puts it, 'So it goes.' "

The best you can hope for is a peaceful, if mutually suspicious, coexistence.

Herein ends the obligatory statement

SOME FINAL OBSERVATIONS ON THE NATURE OF CHANGE

There is one final move I want to make in this book.

I have claimed, repeatedly, that truth changes and that this is a longitudinal study. To be fair about some of the impressions I may have created in the earlier chapters, I want to revisit those locations and see what has happened. What has changed? And what has changed the truth in the tales I have told about them?

A Boston-Based Computer Software Company,
Two Years Later

Let's go back to B-BCSC. When we were there last the culture was in transition. There were only three red cars in the parking lot, and the parking lot was located beyond a sewer drainpipe across the highway from a dive bar and the rest of it.

Things have changed.

Today B-BCSC is located in Research Park West, near a supercomputer facility, down a different divided highway that goes by the name of Discovery Drive. No longer housed in a nondescript building, the new home of B-BCSC is an arresting two-story, mirrored-glass-and-steel structure with white arches and imported marble floors. At night the arches are lit and look like the space shuttle on the launch pad.

When I wrote this piece my method of writing was to move the reader from outside to inside the building, more or less adopting the voice of a knowing tour guide. In part this decision was made because of the structure of the old building, and if I had it to do over again I would have made the same decision. However, the new building does not lend itself to such a pattern of description. I wonder if that would affect what I wrote about, what got noticed, and what significations were suggested by the framework?

The new building evokes in me a different feeling. It is hard to describe because it is simultaneously a modern glass rectangle ripe for New Age music, a religious shrine to the gods of capitalism, and a new place in a recently plowed field where the red dirt of Alabama does not give way easily to manicured lawns. From out front in the red dirt, the sort of red-dirt-and-clay combination that washes across the sidewalk during rainstorms and does not wash off, ever, you can see the super mall rising up behind the new building, separated by a new four-lane divided highway cut from what was once a pleasant stand of old, old hickory and oak trees. In 1987 the local architects' association voted it one of the ten ugliest buildings in Huntsville. But not everyone feels that way.

There have been other changes. Suzi, the receptionist who I believed would always be the receptionist, is no longer a receptionist. She now works in the telephone room answering questions from customers. She was initially replaced by Susan, then Susan moved to the telephone room too. Now, as of this writing, the job is shared by a Mary and a Sandra. There is none of the old feeling here anymore. None of the jokes, either.

Instead we have a surround that I have come to associate with some other new office buildings in Huntsville, particularly firms specializing in computer software and hardware. It is, for lack of a better descriptor, a modified fern bar where the receptionist's area substitutes for the bar and the telephone system substitutes for spirits. There are comfortable chairs and loveseats, suggesting comfortable conversations that do not occur and warm emotions that would there be difficult to express.

It is always medium cool.

The work goes on behind closed doors that limit access from the reception area. If you listen very closely you will here a soft, constant hum of computers and printers, a kind of karmic electric mantra, the postmodern hymn of progress.

Gone were the individualized work spaces, for a while. By company policy. But it did not last very long. Because the furniture was new and expensive, and because there were no walls upon which to hang cartoons, in the beginning only a few symbols remained, mostly objects that could sit quietly on desktops or be put away in drawers. Gone was the sense of individualism that was so much a part of the earlier stage. It was like a theater of absence, where what was missing was the essential clue to what was going on.

Slowly, though, it all came back. In deference to the company policy the B-BCSCers did not so much abandon as redefine the terms of their agreement. Whereas they had previously used all available space for display purposes, in the new building displays are limited to the sharply defined cubicle walls—nothing protrudes above them, hangs out from the sides of them, or is open to view by customers. The individuals reasserted their individualism.

Henry Peppertree is still in charge. These days he receives more criticism at company parties and does not appear to be enjoying it. But that is all right. He has accomplished his job and is still very much the leader. He works with a kind of controlled intensity that inspires confidence but not closeness. Some say he is more interested in playing with the big boys at ZZ than with the locals. In a way he is the hellfire evangelist turned to television personality. Handsome, successful, well-off. No more steak cook-outs. No more experiments.

This is not the same as it was.

The question this raises is unsettling. It is easy for the ethnographer in me to make an argument for the permanence of change. It is quite another matter to spend as much time as I have spent observing, participating, and writing about B-BCSC—trying to find exactly the right voice for what I saw going on there—and then see it all slip away, become a changeling, transform itself into something almost unrecognizable. It is hard to let go.

Yet there is value in it. Organizational studies suffer from the single-snapshot versions of life. We take pictures, develop them, show them to the world, and then act as if the realities we are representing will change no more than photographs change, which is to say, obviously, that they will not change at all. The foci of our observations—in this case the diffusion of innovations born in the firestorm of a change of command— settle down. The processes that created them become increasingly invisible, and the narratives that are told about those times are all that is left. And the narratives lose something too. They have been told and retold and become therefore routinized, little stories well made for an audience ready to be appreciative.

Some other items deserve mention. The woman who was the scapegoat in the original story is a different person. By an act of will, and a transfer to another department, she has become an efficient, goal-oriented, accomplished employee. If I didn't know the history, I wouldn't have a clue to her former identity. Now the scapegoat function seems to have moved from the level of individuals to new technologies that take time to learn and delay schedules and interrupt work routines.

Another change from the original tale is in the parking lot. Gone are two out of the three red cars. Their owners traded them in for other models—the red Alliance for a black Taurus, the red Jetta for a black BMW (actually, the red Jetta was sold to another B-BCSC employee who still has it). Only the red Fiat remains, still not entirely operational, still sporting the same old carburetors. But rumor has it that it is for sale.

New red cars have taken their places.

But something is missing.

In the earlier essay I saw a culture in evolution. It is still evolving, but seems to have reached a kind of plateau of cultural stability where management has replaced leadership and routine has replaced ritual. Gone is the excitement. And the poetry.

Discount Records and Parisian's

Down University Drive about a quarter of a mile from Research Park West is the super mall and beyond it, housed in what is alternately called

Service Merchandise or the Food World shopping center, is the store that used to be called Discount Records.

It is no longer called Discount Records. It is now called Eleanor Rigby's. Turner still works there, however. This is still an intriguing place to observe the identities of the dramatic persona, and aside from the fact that Turner liquidated his rental movie stock and so choices of movies cannot be linked to personalities, everything is the same. This is to say, as I did in the original essay, that you can't step into the same store twice. Which is to say that everything is different. Every experience of consuming is new. You just can't deconstruct the Fishy semiotics of the door anymore.

It's all post-Fish now.

Parisian's, however, is another matter. Since writing the essay I have had two students who worked as clerks in that haven of consumer capitalism. Both of them had "it"—the look of the "Parisian's point of view." When I asked them what that means, they both replied, "Service, PERSONAL Service." They, Both of Them, were in cosmetics. They, Both of Them, plan to go into management. Some things never change.

I discussed my essay with them and was mildly surprised by their responses. They both saw themselves in it, despite the fact that neither of them was. One of them, Pamela, told me that the one thing I left out that should have been included was the cosmetics seminars they attended. I told her I didn't know about them, which was true. She told me that they were told during these seminars that they weren't selling products, they were selling *ideals*. Cultural ideals.

This pleased and disturbed me. It fit perfectly with my observations, but it was far more blatant than I had suspected. Where I had perceived subtlety I now discovered there was none. Pamela went on to describe the cultural ideal as one of image that could be bought for a price. The higher the ideal, the higher the price.

Pamela also told me why my experience of Parisian's had uncovered the "go into management" mentality. As it turns out this is not the myth I had originally read it to be, but a fact. Parisian's has a reputation for training managers. Not just for their own stores, but for other department stores as well. Of course, not everyone who aspires to management eventually arrives there, but some do. And some do in spite of, or perhaps because of, their spelling.

The inside of the store has undergone the usual seasonal changes, but the positions of the merchandise (men on top, women on bottom) have remained the same. The centerpiece still has stairs up to it, but when you get there it is empty. Nothing has yet replaced the once-famous television screens and chocolates. To tell the truth, I miss them.

To write ethnography is to take some chances. You write what you experience and later you wish you had asked more or different questions, paid closer attention to certain details. Such is my feeling about the "Articles of Faith" essay. For example, the comment made by the Clinique girl about "this being just like high school" was used to sum up a perspective on the relations between women and men and their attitudes toward consuming. These days I think it deserved more scrutiny. "High school" is both a cultural metaphor that suggests a time of identity formation and sexual exploration as well as a time when these things actually occur.

Some persons remember high school as something to have survived; others remember it as the source of a lasting sense of fulfillment and happiness; still others remember it with a sentiment akin to Charles Dickens's lines from the beginning of *A Tale of Two Cities:* "It was the best of times, it was the worst of times." These alternative interpretations of the meanings we associate with "high school" might provide critical insights about how a cultural metaphor can be used to study the metaphors of a culture—in this case the metaphors of self, image, consuming, and capitalism.

There is another item of notice in this mall community that escaped commentary during that earlier study. I have learned that "working at the mall" is used as a status statement ("working at Parisian's in the mall" so much the better) in much the same way as "working for IBM." It allows the speaker to derive status from the image of the company instead of from the position he or she actually holds there (shop clerk, accountant, technician, hair stylist). So it seems odd to me that you rarely see a person employed by the mall leaving a job to work for another mall store. When they leave the mall, they leave the entire community. They leave, I think, the *experience* of the mall.

The hardest thing for a Parisian's employee to do on their day off, Pamela told me, was to stay away from the store. Like a Siren, it beckons but must be resisted. So if they shop, they shop elsewhere, and never shop for anything they could buy at Parisian's. This latter sense of loyalty has more to do with how they feel when they consume than the generous employee discount can comfortably account for. Parisian's, it seems, is a source of an irresistible impulse.

Space Camp

Six weeks after we returned from our weekend in Space Camp, the high-ranking university official resigned. Maybe there was a connection.

In the piece I only mention him in passing. I did not write about him as the man who seemed, in his every action, to want this whole thing to work out. *Badly.* I thought about it when I did the writing, but did not include it. It didn't seem connected to anything other than the usual nervousness I have learned to associate with faculty members who are forced to eat with administrators and know they had better enjoy it. Maybe I was wrong.

What this suggests is another problem of writing ethnography. You observe and record but do not always know what to make of your notes. In this case until later. In the meantime you complete the writing. You complete it based on what you thought you saw when you did the observing and recording. You tie it into what seems appropriate or likely. But you are not always right, despite the fact that the printed page makes it seem so.

Frankly, whether or not the high-ranking university official based— even in part—his decision to resign on his Space Camp experiences is still a matter for speculation. During his press conference he told the world that he had made the decision the previous summer on the occasion of his birthday. It is also true that while this information may have altered my perspective a bit, the results of that altering may only have changed a paragraph or two. The rest of it, mostly, still stands.

There have only been two changes.

First, James McPike got tenure! This pleases me.

Second, I read in the newspaper the other day that Space Camp is expanding its operation. More visitors, more young campers, than before. This troubles me. Bring in all the adults you want to, but please leave the children alone. They have so few defenses, and they are so easily impressed by uniforms and video games, the glitter and suck of technology.

Star Wars

One of the most interesting changes to have taken place in this community since I examined the Strategic Defense Command headquarters is the public relations about it.

During the time of my study it was still a kind of community secret, something hidden from common knowledge. However, ever since the increased communication between the Soviets and us about Star Wars research programs, the store of common knowledge expanded.

It began with the thirtieth anniversary of Army missile research, an event marked by an "open house" at SDC and a full week of heavy local news coverage. Actually, it began long before that, during the planning sessions that preceded the event. For weeks prior to the event there would be the occasional news story about the successes of the Star Wars program. They were small successes told in a BIG WAY. There was also the surround created by Prime Minister Gorbachev and President Reagan's discussions of the missile reduction treaties that featured Star Wars in the headlines. But it was the week of the "open house" at the room where the end of the world was planned that focused local attention on this local enterprise

One of the curious features of the open house was the fact that it was open. It really was *open*. Visitors were given the whole tour, shown the simulation room, and invited to inspect the printouts while their uniformed guide smiled and spoke softly about its deterrent effects. However open the appearance, there were no printouts with bad news on them. Every scenario depicted the ability of the three layers of Star Wars defenses to completely control a nuclear attack. This was contrary both to my previous research and to the opinions of persons who worked there; it reminded me of David Stockman's notorious statement about computerized budgets: "If you don't like the numbers, change the formulas."

I think the formulas changed.

Too much was staged. People smiled.

Visitors were also given the usual propaganda in the form of booklets on the (selective) history of missile research, booklets that detail who was in charge of the various research programs and the success of tests, but contain very little other information. Visitors were also not shown the work of the SDC public relations office in collecting anti-SDI literatures from around the world, and their various strategic responses to them. For example, every cartoon that has a negative SDI message is filed. When deemed appropriate, a letter to the editor or another, perhaps more subtle form of persuasion is generated back to its source.

Are cartoons a threat to the defense of the country? I think not. It is frightening to think that such information is regularly and routinely collected and filed in some government repository where it is readily available for uses against American citizens. I weep, still, for the defense of my country, for its loss of democratic ideals, for its passive acceptance of such tyranny.

This is the one essay in this collection that I would not change if I had it to do over again. However, with it behind me I would love to pursue one of the persistent questions raised by this investigation—what sort of culture (or perhaps, to borrow Gareth Morgan's metaphor, psychic prison) is created under conditions like these? Most of the people who work there don't believe their product can work, and (I hope) none of them ever wants to see it used. Clearly this is not a habitat for the typical American worker or manager. It deserves further study.

CONCLUSIONS

I came into this project with multiple senses of purpose.

I knew I wanted to understand some of the connections between culture, technology, and communication. I knew also that I wanted to display aspects of those cultural ingredients that seemed to support the consensus reality that was so much a natural part of this environment. It was like looking at one large, ongoing, but highly differentiated ritual.

I suspected that technology was an extension of the machine. Having done some necessary reading in the history of technology I had learned that progress had led us from the mechanical age to the electrical age, and that our development, diffusion, and uses of the electronic and the digital could be explained by a linear sort of logic. In hindsight I believe this assumption is wrong.

Although you can see how reasoning figured into the processes that led us from catapults to air balloons to multiple-warhead nuclear missiles, to read history that way is to embed within the text a source of delusion. Similarly, to read the history of office automation as a steady stream of improvements that replaced pen and ink with typewriters, then with self-correcting typewriters, then with computers, is to misread that history, to see it as a history of improvements rather than the gradual imposition of a new way of life on the already living.

The new technology is different form the machines that preceded it. A machine is under the control of its operators and does not encourage dependence so much as cooperation. Technology, on the other hand, may be directed by its operators, but is seldom under their control. We use computers, but aside from the language we have acquired to describe how they work we have no ability to repair them. And in fact, repairs are not always necessary. If you own a computer that is more than five years old and it still works properly, then chances are that when it ceases to function you will be encouraged to consume a new one rather than try to repair the old one. The technology has changed, improved, and you will have little choice because nothing is less valued in a technological society than old technology. The circuit boards—called, interestingly enough, motherboards—will no longer be manufactured. Your "mother" is dead and there is faceless Technology dominating your life, requiring dependence.

This brings me to what is perhaps the most arresting point. Machines may break, but technology *fails*. The world within these words is important because it points to, signifies, a broader cultural context already embedded within its meanings. Consider the case of the broken typewriter, and all that it implies. Let's say the keys stick. Although you can unstick the keys yourself and if necessary fiddle with the internal mechanism, you decide instead to take it to the shop for repairs. There a knowledgeable person fixes the problem, either by replacing a worn piece or perhaps simply by lubricating the mechanism. You pick it up, go back to work. At most you've lost some time and spent a little money. But the machine functions perfectly and does not require additional discussion. You are free to go to a Springsteen concert, if you wish.

By contrast, let's assume it isn't the mechanical age anymore, and instead of keys sticking on a typewriter you find a bureaucracy that encourages cover-ups instead of disclosure. Perhaps this is an unfair analogy, but bear with me. Before, the typewriter was a machine that was used to do something else—to make a product, send a bill, write poetry. Now, bureaucracy is in the service of technology—the force behind the launch of missiles, for instance. When these keys stick, as they did during the *Challenger* disaster, the result is not a broken machine that can be fixed but a failed technology that, after its moment of fire and flames and human destruction, demands to be replaced. Moreover, when technology fails there is no going to the concert. Your attention, your discussions, your sense of purpose are tied to the failure. Everything else recedes, becomes less important. What can poetry do about that? What is the point of interpretive ethnography?

There are sticky keys, and then there are STICKY KEYS!

Technology is born of an engineering mentality. It is, as many observers have pointed out, a mentality of cause and effect, of on or off, a linear and dichotomous logic that values what can be done over the ethics and morality of the processes necessary to produce it. It is no accident, I think, that engineers and entrepreneurs flock to high-technology environments and gaggle there. Nor is it an accident that persons who practice the arts and sciences in these regions are defined as lesser humans, worth less money, good only for the practical applications of whatever they claim to be doing. Nor is it an accident that when "accidents" happen, the persons most likely to offer a fresh perspective on the problem are the least likely to be invited to the table. Where were the independent philosophers and scientists, or for that matter the organizational communication scholars, during the *Challenger* hearings?

Like Humpty-Dumpty, when technology fails all the king's horses and all the king's men cannot put poor Humpty together again. Theirs are the tools and the languages of the solution to the problem that did not solve the problem, but instead created a much larger one. Technology did not replace the machine; it abandoned it in favor of an entirely new system, a much larger and potentially more totalitarian one.

There is a language fostered by a high-technology culture that shows up in the talk of members of the culture and forms intricate curves in its rituals of conversation. Unlike previous machine-oriented or even agriculturally-oriented cultures, ignorance of how something works does not carry with it any stigma. In a high-technology culture it is okay to be dumb about technologies that do not support your work environment, to express that sentiment thusly: "I don't want to know *how* it works, I just want it to work." Here again, technology fosters dependence, separates us even further from the know-how that defined the can-do generation. Supported by the intoxicating spirits of consumer capitalism—hyper-capitalism—and the language of consensus delusion, the answer to any failure of technology is simply to spend more money and buy its newest replacement.

I just used the term "delusion" for the second time. The delusion I am speaking of here is one of Progress, defined by the bright promise of words such as "new," "better," and "best," shaped by the forces of technological improvements and guided by the consistent presence of the hunger to consume that directs its intelligence toward acquiring and spending money. This is the verbal diet of a technological society that sees its ideal image in that which it can never fully attain, and punishes itself for its longing.

Within this culture there is little appreciation for questions or criticism. These are the vocabularies of the opposition, the other side of the dichotomous world that lives only in its own delusion. For within a technological culture, perhaps and particularly one driven by the engines of the military, life is a battle between opposing sides, and what is "right" is less important than being loyal. Arguments are perceived as weapons capable of mutually assured destruction, and so they are feared and avoided. What is valued in this mini-Republic is strict adherence to the first principles of delusion: that money is the reason why we live the way we do, that power is a function of money, that seniority is more important than talent or initiative, and that who we are and what we are worth as human beings is entirely dependent on the status of where we work, and that everything else is bullshit.

This is a dangerous place, the cutting edge of a new version of America. It is a text that reads like a science that hopes to become science fiction. Embedded within the text are emblems of a history and literature of America that is forgotten and a future that trades away personal dignity and imagination for the surface appeal of the cosmetic and fashionable, that gives away personal identity in exchange for nothing at all.

Technology is sorcery, word-magic, the secret tongues of a burgeoning civil religion. It is something its adherents *believe in* rather than do. Its source of mystery is always derived from the fear that some bigger, better Technology is out there waiting to be discovered, bringing with it riches and power beyond our wildest dreams. Technology therefore devalues all other religions, all other sources of faith. Ironically, it fits perfectly into the sense of religion that is founded upon the rock of big business, the religion that promises an enjoyable (one imagines profitable) afterlife in exchange for a share of your present earnings, the laying on of hands among those who truly tithe.

But we cannot live without it. We must remember that.

Technology will not go away, nor will it turn back on itself, nor will it become more open to criticism. We have become too dependent upon it and besides, the world is too fast and threatening a place for us without it. Like the age-old questions about poverty that Tolstoy asks, just throwing our money at the poor will not solve the problem. Nor will throwing away technology. It rides along with us on this darkening star, already moving at speed toward some random place.

Our task is to make the place less random.

This is where this book ends.

This is where the detective turns out the lights, notices that it is later than he thought, and decides to stop somewhere for a sandwich and a beer before making his way home. Going down the steps and out the door he thinks about all of those dreams he had as a kid about what his life would be like. He chuckles.

Turns up the collar on his raincoat.

And winks, directly at you.

Influences

Influences

Agar, M. 1980. *The professional stranger*. New York: Academic Press.
———. 1982. Toward an ethnographic language. *American Anthropologist* 84: 779–95.
———. 1986. *Speaking of ethnography*. Beverly Hills, Calif.: Sage.
Allaire, Y., and M. E. Firsirotu. 1984. Theories of organizational culture. *Organization Studies* 5: 193–226.
Altick, R. D. [1950] 1987. *The scholar adventurers*. Columbus: Ohio State University Press.
Arac, J. 1986. *Postmodernism and politics*. Minneapolis: University of Minnesota Press.
Ardrey, R. 1967. *The territorial imperative*. New York: Atheneum.
———. 1970. *The social contract*. New York: Atheneum.
Aristotle. 1954. *The rhetoric and poetics*. Trans. W. R. Roberts. New York: Modern Library.
Astley, W. G. 1985. Administrative science as socially-constructed truth. *Administrative Science Quarterly* 30: 497–513.
Ballard, E. G. 1978. *Man and technology: Toward the measurement of a culture*. Pittsburgh: Duquesne University Press.
Barney, J. B. 1986. Organizational culture: Can it be a source of sustained competitive advantage. *Academy of Management Review* 11: 656–65.
Barrett, W. 1978. *The illusion of technique: A search for meaning in a technological civilization*. Garden City, N.Y.: Doubleday/Anchor.
———. 1986. *Death of the soul: From Descartes to the computer*. Garden City, N.Y.: Doubleday/Anchor.
Barthes, R. 1972. *Mythologies*. New York: Hill & Wang.
———. 1979. *A lover's discourse: Fragments*. Trans. R. Howard. New York: Hill & Wang.
Bateson, G. 1936. *Naven*. Stanford, Calif.: Stanford University Press.
Becker, E. 1962. *The birth and death of meaning*. New York: Free Press.
Becker, H. S. 1986. *Writing for social scientists*. Chicago: University of Chicago Press.
Bell, D. 1976. *The cultural contradictions of capitalism*. New York: Basic Books.
Benamou, M. 1980. Notes on the technological imagination. In *Technological imagination: Theories and fictions,* ed. T. DeLauretis, A. Huyscn, and K. Woodward. Madison, Wis.: Coda Press.
Benson, J. K. 1977. Innovation and crisis in organizational analysis. *Sociological Quarterly* 18: 3–16.
———. 1977. Organizations: A dialectical view. *Administrative Science Quarterly* 22: 1–21.
Benson, T. 1981. Another shootout in cowtown. *Quarterly Journal of Speech* 67: 347–406.
Berger, P. L., and T. Luckmann. 1967. *The social construction of reality*. Garden City, N.Y.: Doubleday/Anchor.
Bernal, J. D. 1971. *Science in history*. 4 vols. Cambridge, Mass.: M.I.T. Press.

Bernstein, B. 1964. Elaborated and restricted codes. *American Anthropologist* 66: 55–69.

Bersheid, E., and E. H. Walster. 1978. *Interpersonal attraction.* 2d. ed. Reading, Mass.: Addison-Wesley.

Beyer, J. M., and H. M. Trice. 1987. How an organization's rites reveal its culture. *Organizational Dynamics* 15: 4–25.

Bhagat, R. S., and S. J. McQuaid. 1982. Role of subjective culture in organizations: A review and directions for future research. *Journal of Applied Psychology* 67: 653–85.

Bok, S. 1983. *Secrets: On the ethics of concealment and revelation.* New York: Pantheon.

Boorstin, D. J. 1978. *The republic of technology: Reflections on our future community.* New York: Harper & Row.

———. [1961] 1987. *The image: A guide to pseudo-events in America.* New York: Atheneum.

Borgmann, A. 1984. *Technology and the character of contemporary life: A philosophical inquiry.* Chicago: University of Chicago Press.

Bormann, E. G. 1972. Fantasy and rhetorical vision: The rhetorical criticism of social reality. *Quarterly Journal of Speech* 58: 396–407.

———. 1982. Symbolic convergence theory of communication: Applications and implications for teachers and consultants. *Journal of Applied Communication Research* 10: 50–61.

———. 1983. Symbolic convergence: Organizational communication and culture. In *Communication and organization: An interpretive approach,* ed. L. L. Putnam and M. E. Pacanowsky. Beverly Hills, Calif.: Sage.

Broms, H., and H. Gahmberg. 1983. Communication to self in organizations and cultures. *Administrative Science Quarterly* 28: 482–95.

Bronowski, J. 1974. *The ascent of man.* Boston: Little, Brown.

Brown, R. H. 1977. *A poetic for sociology.* Cambridge: Cambridge University Press.

Browning, L. D. 1978. A grounded organizational communication theory derived from qualitative data. *Communication Monographs* 45: 93–109.

Bruner, E. M. 1986. Ethnography as narrative. In *The anthropology of experience,* ed. V. T. Turner and E. M. Bruner. Urbana: University of Illinois Press.

Burke, K. [1924] 1968. *The complete white oxen.* Berkeley: University of California Press.

———. [1931] 1968. *Counter-statement.* Berkeley: University of California Press.

———. [1932] 1982. *Towards a better life.* Berkeley: University of California Press.

———. [1935] 1965. *Permanence and change,* 2d. rev. ed. Indianapolis: Bobbs-Merrill.

———. [1941] 1967. *The philosophy of literary form.* Berkeley: University of California Press.

———. [1945] 1969. *A grammar of motives.* Berkeley: University of California Press.

———. [1950] 1969. *A rhetoric of motives.* Berkeley: University of California Press.

———. [1961] 1970. *The rhetoric of religion: Studies in logology.* Berkeley: University of California Press.

———. 1966. *Language as symbolic action: Essays on life, literature, and method.* Berkeley: University of California Press.

———. 1982. Burke on Burke. Talk presented at the Eastern Communication Association convention, Hartford, Connecticut, April.

Burrell, G., and G. Morgan. 1979. *Sociological paradigms and organizational analysis.* London: Heinemann.

Calas, M. B., and L. Smircich. 1987. Post-culture: Is the organizational culture literature dominant but dead? Paper presented at the Third International Conference on Organizational Symbolism and Corporate Culture, Milan, Italy, June.

———. 1987. Reading leadership as a form of cultural analysis. In *Emerging leadership vistas,* ed. J. L. Hunt, R. Baliga, C. Schriesheim, and P. Dachler. Lexington, Mass.: Lexington Books.

Carbaugh, D. 1988. Cultural terms and tensions in the speech at a television station. *Western Journal of Speech Communication* 52: 216–37.

Carpenter, H. 1978. *Shopping center management.* New York: International Council of Shopping Centers.

Cassirer, E. [1944] 1978. *An essay on man.* New Haven, Conn.: Yale University Press.

———. [1946] 1971. *The myth of state.* New Haven, Conn.: Yale University Press.

Cawelti, J. G. 1976. *Adventure, mystery, and romance: Formula stories as art and popular culture.* Chicago: University of Chicago Press.

Cawelti, J. G., and B. A. Rosenberg. 1987. *The spy story.* Chicago: University of Chicago Press.

Chandler, Raymond. 1939. *The big sleep.* New York: Knopf.

———. 1940. *Farewell, my lovely.* New York: Knopf.

———. 1942. *The high window.* New York: Knopf.

———. 1943. *The lady in the lake.* New York: Knopf.

———. 1949. *The little sister.* New York: Random House.

———. 1950. *The simple art of murder.* New York: Houghton Mifflin.

———. 1953. *The long goodbye.* New York: Random House.

———. 1958. *Playback.* New York: Random House.

———. 1964. *Killer in the rain.* New York: Random House.

———. 1965. *The smell of fear.* New York: Random House.

Cheney, G. 1983. On the various and changing meanings of organizational membership. *Communication Monographs* 50: 342–62.

———. 1983. The rhetoric of identification and the study of organizational communication. *Quarterly Journal of Speech* 69: 143–58.

Chesebro, J. W. 1984. The media reality: Epistemological functions of media in cultural systems. *Critical Studies in Mass Communication* 1: 111–30.

Clifford, J., and G. E. Marcus, eds. 1986. *Writing culture: The poetics and politics of ethnography.* Berkeley: University of California Press.

Cohen, S., and L. Taylor. 1978. *Escape attempts: The theory and practice of resistance to everyday life.* New York: Penguin.

Conklin, H. 1968. Ethnography. In *International encyclopedia of social science,* ed. D. E. Sills. Vol. 5. New York: Free Press.

Conrad, C. 1984. Phases, pentads, and dramatistic critical process. *Central States Speech Journal* 34: 94–104.

———. 1985. *Strategic organizational communication.* New York: Holt.

———. 1985. Chrysanthemums and swords: A reading of contemporary organizational communication theory and research. *The Southern Speech Communication Journal* 50: 189–200.

Cragan, J. F., and D. C. Shields 1981. *Applied communication research: A dramatistic approach.* Prospect Heights, Ill.: Waveland Press.

Crowley, D. J. 1982. *Understanding communication: The signifying web.* New York: Gordon and Breach.

Culler, J. 1982. *On deconstruction: Theory and criticism after structuralism.* Ithaca, N.Y.: Cornell University Press.

Currie-McDaniel, R. 1987. *The U. S. Army Strategic Defense Command: Its history and role in the strategic defense iniative.* Huntsville, Ala.: Historical Office, U. S. Army Strategic Defense Command.

Daft, R. L., and J. C. Wiginton. 1979. Language and organization. *Academy of Management Review* 4: 179–91.

Dandridge, T. C., I. I. Mitroff, and W. F. Joyce. 1980. Organizational symbolism: A topic to expand organizational analysis. *Academy of Management Review* 5: 77–82.

Daniels, T., and K. Frandsen. 1984. Conventional social science inquiry in human communication theory and practice. *Quarterly Journal of Speech* 70: 223–40.

Davis, K. 1953. Management communication and the grapevine. *Harvard Business Review* 31: 43–49.

———. 1978. Methods for studying informal communication. *Journal of Communication* 28: 112–16.

Davis, W. 1985. *The serpent and the rainbow.* New York: Simon & Schuster.

Deal, T. E., and A. A. Kennedy. 1982. *Corporate cultures: The rites and rituals of corporate life.* Reading, Mass.: AddisonWesley.

Deetz, S. A. 1982. Critical interpretive research in organizational communication. *Western Journal of Speech Communication* 46: 131–49.

———. 1984. Metaphors and the discursive production and reproduction of organization. In *People, communication, and organizational performance,* ed. L. Thayer and O. Wiio. New York: Ablex.

Dégerardo, J.-M. [1800] 1969. *The observation of savage peoples.* Trans. F. C. T. Moore. Berkeley: University of California Press.

Derrida, J. 1974. *Of grammatology.* Baltimore: Johns Hopkins University Press.

Dillon, G. L. 1986. *Rhetoric as social imagination: Explorations in the interpersonal function of language.* Bloomington: University of Indiana Press.

Dollars and cents of shopping centers 1981. Washington, D.C.: Urban Land Institute.

Drucker, P. 1977. *Technology, management, and society.* New York: Harper & Row.

Duncan, H. D. 1962. *Communication and social order.* New York: Oxford University Press.

———. 1968. *Symbols in society.* New York: Oxford University Press.

Eco, U. 1976. *A theory of semiotics.* Bloomington: Indiana University Press.

———. 1977. *Semiotics of theatrical performance.* Bloomington: Indiana University Press.

Edelman, M. 1971. *Politics as symbolic action.* New York: Academic Press.

———. 1977. *Political language: Words that succeed and politics that fail.* New York: Academic Press.

Eisenberg, E. M. 1984. Ambiguity as strategy in organizational communication. *Communication Monographs* 51: 227–42.

———. 1987. Reconsidering openness in organizational communication. *Academy of Management Review* 12: 418–26.

Eisenberg, E. M., and P. R. Riley. 1988. Symbols and sense-making in organizations. In *Handbook of organizational communication,* ed. G. Goldhaber. Norwood, N.J.: Ablex.

Ellis, D. G. 1980. Ethnographic considerations in initial interactions. *Western Journal of Speech Communication* 44: 104–7.

Ellul, J. 1964. *The technological society.* New York: Knopf.

———. 1980. The power of technique and the ethics of non- power. In *The myths of information: Technology and postindustrial culture,* ed. K. Woodward. Madison, Wis.: Coda Press.

Etzioni, A. 1964. *Modern organizations.* Englewood Cliffs, N.J.: Prentice-Hall.

———. 1968. *The active society.* New York: Free Press.

Evans-Pritchard, E. E. 1936. *Witchcraft, oracles, and magic among the Azande.* Oxford: Oxford University Press.

———. 1940. *The Neur.* Oxford: Oxford University Press.

————. 1973. Some reminiscences and reflections on fieldwork. *Journal of the Anthropological Society of Oxford* 4: 1–12.

Falk, E. H. 1967. *Types of thematic structures.* Chicago: University of Chicago Press.

Farace, R., P. Monge, and H. Russell. 1977. *Communication in organizations.* Reading, Mass.: Addison-Wesley.

Farrell, T. B. 1976. Knowledge, consensus, and rhetorical theory. *Quarterly Journal of Speech* 62: 1–14.

————. 1978. Social knowledge II. *Quarterly Journal of Speech* 64: 329–34.

Farrell, T. B., and G. T. Goodnight. 1981. Accidental rhetoric: The root metaphors of Three Mile Island. *Communication Monographs* 48: 271–300.

Feldman, M. S., and J. G. March. 1981. Information in organizations as signal and symbol. *Administrative Science Quarterly* 26: 171–86.

Fish, S. 1979. Normal circumstances, literal language, direct speech acts, the ordinary, the everyday, the obvious, what goes without saying, and other special cases. In *Interpretive social science: A reader,* ed. P. Rabinow and W. M. Sullivan. Berkeley: University of California Press.

Fisher, W. R. 1984. Narration as a human communication paradigm: The case of public moral argument. *Communication Monographs* 51: 1–22.

Fitzgerald, F. S. [1925] 1953. *The great Gatsby.* New York: Charles Scribner's Sons.

Fletcher, C. 1981. *The man from the cave.* New York: Random House.

Flink, J. J. 1975. *The car culture.* Cambridge, Mass.: M.I.T. Press.

Foster, H. 1983. *The anti-aesthetic: Essays on postmodern culture.* Port Townsend, Wash.: Bay Press.

Foucalt, M. 1972. *The archaeology of knowledge.* New York: Pantheon.

————. 1973. *The order of things.* New York: Vintage.

————. 1976. *Discipline and punish.* New York: Vintage.

————. 1977. *Language, counter-memory, practice.* Ithaca, N.Y.: Cornell University Press.

Freeman, D. 1983. *Margaret Mead and Samoa.* Cambridge: Harvard University Press.

Frentz, T. S., and T. B. Farrell. 1976. Language-action: A paradigm for communication. *Quarterly Journal of Speech* 62: 333–49.

Frost, P. J., L. F. Moore, M. R. Louis, C. C. Lundberg, and J. Martin. 1985. *Organizational Culture.* Beverly Hills, Calif.: Sage.

Galbraith, J. K. 1967. *The new industrial state.* Boston: Houghton-Mifflin.

Garfinkel, H. 1967. *Studies in ethnomethodology.* Englewood Cliffs, N.J.: Prentice-Hall.

Geertz, C. 1973. *The interpretation of culture.* New York: Basic Books.

————. 1983. *Local knowledge.* New York: Basic Books.

————. 1988. *Works and lives: The anthropologist as author.* Palo Alto, Calif.: Stanford University Press.

Giddens, A. 1979. *Central problems in social theory.* Berkeley: University of California Press.

Glaser, B., and A. Strauss. 1967. *The discovery of grounded theory.* Chicago: Aldine.

Goffman, E. 1959. *The presentation of self in everyday life.* Garden City, N.Y.: Doubleday/ Anchor Books.

————. 1961. *Encounters.* Indianapolis: Bobbs Merrill.

————. 1963. *Behavior in public places.* New York: Free Press.

————. 1967. *Interaction ritual.* New York: Doubleday/ Anchor.

————. 1971. *Relations in public.* New York: Basic Books.

————. 1974. *Frame analysis: An essay on the organization of experience.* New York: Harper & Row.

————. 1981. *Forms of talk.* Philadelphia: University of Pennsylvania Press.

————. 1983. The interaction order. *American Sociological Review* 48: 1–17.

Goldman, A. 1976. Do lower-income customers have a more restricted shopping scope? *Journal of Marketing* 40: 46–54.

Goldzwig, S., and G. N. Dionisopoulos. 1986. Explaining it to ourselves: The phases of national mourning in space tragedy. *Central States Speech Journal* 37: 180–92.

Goodall, Jr., H. L. 1983. The nature of analogic discourse. *Quarterly Journal of Speech* 69: 171–79.

————. 1984. *Small group communication in organizations*. Dubuque, Iowa: William C. Brown.

————. 1984. The status of communication studies in organizational contexts: One rhetorician's lament after a year-long odyssey. *Communication Quarterly* 32: 133–47.

————. 1984. Research priorities for investigations of gender and communication: Rediscovering the human experience of sexuality and talk. *Women's Studies in Communication* 7: 91–97.

————. 1986. Review of Wade Davis's *The serpent and the rainbow*. *Southern Speech Communication Journal* 51: 250–52.

————. 1987. Performance appraisal reviews in academic settings: Two problems, one lesson, and a moral. *ACA Bulletin* 61: 50–60.

Goodall, Jr., H. L., and M. J. Hyde. 1983. The influences of technology on human communication. *Communication Quarterly* 32. Special issue.

Goodall, Jr., H. L., and G. M. Phillips 1981. Assumption of the burden: Science or criticism? *Communication Quarterly* 29: 282–96.

————. 1984. *Making it in any organization*. Englewood Cliffs, N.J.: Prentice- Hall/ Spectrum Books.

Goodall, Jr., H. L., G. L. Wilson, and C. L. Waagen. 1986. The performance appraisal interview: An interpretive reassessment. *Quarterly Journal of Speech* 72: 74–87.

Goodenough, W. H. 1971. *Culture, language, and society*. Reading, Mass.: Addison-Wesley.

Gouran, D. S., R. Y. Hirokawa, and A. E. Martz. 1986. A critical analysis of factors related to decisional processes involved in the *Challenger* disaster. *Central States Speech Journal* 37: 119–35.

Graff, G. 1979. *Literature against itself*. Chicago: University of Chicago Press.

Gray, B., M. Bougon, and A. Donnellon. 1985. Organizations as constructions and destructions of meaning. *Journal of Management* 11: 83–98.

Gregory, K. L. 1983. Native-view paradigms: Multiple cultures and culture conflicts in organizations. *Administrative Science Quarterly* 28: 359–76.

Gruen, V., and L. Smith. 1960. *Shopping towns USA: The planning of shopping centers*. Chicago: Reinhold.

Guetzkow, H. 1965. Communication in organizations. In *Handbook of organizations*, ed. J. March. Chicago: Rand-McNally.

Gusfield, J. 1981. *The culture of public problems*. Chicago: University of Chicago Press.

Haley, J. 1963. *Strategies of psychotherapy*. New York: Grune and Stratton.

————. 1973. *Uncommon therapy*. New York: Norton.

————. 1976. *Problem-solving therapy*. New York: Harper & Row.

Hall, E. T. 1959. *The silent language*. Garden City, N.Y.: Doubleday.

————. 1977. *Beyond culture*. Garden City, N.Y.: Doubleday/Anchor.

————. 1978. Autonomy and dependence in technological environments: Review and commentary. In *Communication Yearbook 2*, ed. B. Rubin, 23–28. New Brunswick, N.J.: ICA/Transaction Books.

Halloran, M. S. 1978. Eloquence in a technological society. *Central States Speech Journal* 29: 221–27.

Hammett, D. 1929. *The Dain curse*. New York: Knopf.

——. 1929. *Red harvest*. New York: Knopf.

——. 1930. *The Maltese falcon*. New York: Knopf.

——. 1931. *The glass key*. New York: Knopf.

——. 1934. *The thin man*. New York: Knopf.

Hampton-Turner, C. 1981. *Maps of the mind*. New York: Macmillan.

Hannah, B. 1973. *Geronimo rex*. New York: Viking.

——. 1974. *Nightwatchmen*. New York: Viking.

——. 1978. *Airships*. New York: Knopf.

——. 1980. *Ray*. New York: Knopf.

——. 1983. *The tennis handsome*. New York: Knopf.

——. 1985. *Captain Maximus*. New York: Knopf.

——. 1987. *Hey Jack!* New York: E. P. Dutton/Seymour Lawrence.

Harari, J. V., ed. 1979. *Textual Strategies: Perspectives in post-structuralist criticism*. Ithaca, N.Y.: Cornell University Press.

Harper's Index, 1987. New York: Harper's Magazine Press.

Harre, R. 1979. *Social being*. Oxford: Basil Blackwell.

Harre, R., and P. F. Secord. 1972. *The explanation of social behaviour*. Oxford: Basil Blackwell.

Hassan, I. 1975. *Paracriticism*. Urbana: University of Illinois Press.

——. 1982. *The dismemberment of Orpheus: Toward a postmodern literature*. 2d. ed. Madison: University of Wisconsin Press.

Hassan, I., and S. Hassan. 1983. *Innovation/Renovation*. Madison: University of Wisconsin Press.

Hawes, L. C. 1974. Social collectivities as communication: Perspectives on organizational behavior. *The Quarterly Journal of Speech* 60: 497–502.

——. 1977. *The pragmatics of analoguing*. Reading, Mass.: Addison-Wesley.

——. 1977. Toward a hermeneutic phenomenology of communication. *Communication Quarterly* 25: 30–41.

——. 1978. The reflexivity of communication research. *Western Journal of Speech Communication* 42: 12–20.

——. 1986. The culture of addiction. Paper presented at the Interpretive Approaches to the Study of Organizations conference, Alta, Utah, August.

Hawes, L. C., and D. H. Smith. 1973. A critique of assumptions underlying the study of communication in conflict. *Quarterly Journal of Speech* 59: 423–35.

Henry, J. 1963. *Culture against man*. New York: Random House.

Hickson III, M. 1983. Ethnomethodology: The promise of applied communication research? *Southern Speech Communication Journal* 48: 182–95.

Hirsch, E. D. 1987. *Cultural literacy*. New York: Basic Books.

Hyde, M. J., ed. 1982. *Communication philosophy and the technological age*. University: University of Alabama Press.

Hymes, D. 1962. The ethnography of speaking. In *Anthropology and Human Behavior*, ed. T. Gladwin and W. Sturtevant. Washington, D.C.: Anthropological Society of Washington.

Jablin, F. M. 1982. Formal structural characteristics of organizations and superior-subordinate communication. *Human Communication Research* 8: 338–47.

————. 1985. An exploratory study of vocational organizational communication socialization. *Southern Speech Communication Journal* 50: 262–82.

Jacobs, J. 1984. *The mall: An attempted escape from everyday life.* Prospect Heights, Ill.: Waveland Press.

Jameson, F. 1984. Postmodernism, or the cultural logic of late capitalism. *New Left Review* 146: 53–92.

————. 1984. The politics of theory: Positions in the postmodernism debate. *New German Critique* 33: 53–65.

Jelinek, M., L. Smircich, and P. Hirsch, eds. 1983. Organizational culture. *Administrative Science Quarterly* 28. Special Issue.

Jermier, J. M. 1985. "When the sleeper wakes": A short story extending themes in radical organization theory. *Journal of Management* 11: 67–80.

Johnson, B. M. 1977. *Communication: The process of organizing.* Boston: Allyn & Bacon.

Jung, C. G. 1962. The unconscious mind. *The Atlantic Monthly,* Dec.

Kafka, F. [1926]; 1958. *The castle.* New York: Schocken Books.

————. [1937]; 1968. *The trial.* New York: Schocken Books.

Kantner, R. M. 1977. *Men and women of the corporation.* New York: Basic Books.

Katriel, T., and G. Philipsen. 1981. "What we need is communication": "Communication" as a cultural category in some American speech. *Communication Monographs* 48: 301–17.

Kets de Vries, M., and D. Miller. *The neurotic organization.* San Francisco: Jossey-Bass.

————. 1986. Personality, culture, and organization. *Academy of Management Review* 11: 266–79.

Kidder, T. 1981. *The soul of a new machine.* Boston: Little, Brown.

Kilmann, R., M. Saxton, and R. Serpa. 1985. *Gaining Control of the Corporate Culture.* San Francisco: Jossey-Bass.

Koch, S., and S. Deetz. 1981. Metaphor analysis of social reality in organizations. *Journal of Applied Communication Research* 9: 1–15.

Korzybski, A. 1933. *Science and sanity.* Lancaster, Penna.: Science Press.

Kowinski, W. S. 1985. *The malling of America: An inside look at the great consumer paradise.* New York: Morrow.

Kramer, M. 1983. *Invasive procedures.* New York: Harper & Row.

Kuhn, T. S. [1962]; 1970. *The structure of scientific revolutions.* 2d. ed. Chicago: University of Chicago Press.

Lacan, J. 1966. *Ecrits.* Paris: Seuil.

————. 1968. *The language of the self: The function of language in psychoanalysis.* Baltimore: Johns Hopkins University Press.

Laing, R. D. 1965. *The divided self.* Harmondsworth, Eng.: Penguin.

Lakoff, G. 1987. *Women, fire, and dangerous things.* Chicago: University of Chicago Press.

————, and M. Johnson 1980. *Metaphors we live by.* Chicago: University of Chicago Press.

Lanser, S. S. 1981. *The narrative act: Point of view in prose fiction.* Princeton, N.J.: Princeton University Press.

Lévi-Strauss, C. 1963. *Structural anthropology.* Trans. C. Jacobson and B. G. Schoepf. New York: Basic Books.

————. 1966. *The savage mind.* New York: Free Press.

Le Vot, A. [1979] 1983. *F. Scott Fitzgerald: A biography.* Trans. W. Byron. New York: Doubleday.

Lewin, K. 1951. *Field theory in social science.* New York: Harper.

Lewis, D. L., and L. Goldstine, eds. 1980. *The automobile and American culture.* Ann Arbor: University of Michigan Press.

Lincoln, Y. S., ed. 1985. *Organizational theory and inquiry: The paradigm revolution.* Beverly Hills, Calif.: Sage.

Lofland, J. 1976. *Doing social life.* New York: Wiley.

Louis, M. L. 1980. "Surprise and sense-making: What newcomers experience in entering unfamiliar organizational settings." *Administrative Science Quarterly* 23: 225–51.

Lurie, A. 1981. *The language of clothes.* New York: Random House.

Lyotard, J. F. 1984. *The postmodern condition: A report on knowledge.* Minneapolis: University of Minnesota Press.

McCloskey, D. N. 1985. *The rhetoric of economics.* Madison: University of Wisconsin Press.

McInerney, J. 1984. *Bright lights, big city.* New York: Vintage.

———. 1985. *Ransom.* New York: Vintage.

McLuhan, M. 1964. *Understanding media.* New York: McGraw-Hill.

McLuhan, M., and Fiore, Q. 1967. *The medium is the massage.* New York: Bantam.

McNeill, W. H. 1982. *The pursuit of power: Technology, armed force, and society since* A.D. 1000. Chicago: University of Chicago Press.

McPhee, R. D., and P. K. Tompkins. 1985. *Organizational communication: Traditional themes and new directions.* Beverly Hills, Calif.: Sage.

MacShane, F. 1976. *The life of Raymond Chandler.* New York: Dutton.

Malinowski, B. 1935. *Coral gardens and their magic.* New York: American Books.

———. [1922] 1961. *Argonauts of the Western Pacific.* New York: Dutton.

———. 1967. *A diary in the strict sense of the term.* New York: Harcourt, Brace, & World.

Mangham, I. L., and M. A. Overington. 1987. *Organizations as theatre: A social psychology of dramatic appearances.* New York: Wiley.

Manning, P. K. 1979. Metaphors of the field. *Administrative Science Quarterly* 24: 425–41.

———. 1987. *Semiotics and fieldwork.* Beverly Hills, Calif.: Sage.

Marcus, G. E. 1980. Rhetoric and the ethnographic genre in anthropological research. *Current Anthropology* 21: 507–10.

Marcus, G. E., and R. Cushman. 1982. Ethnographies as texts. *Annual Review of American Anthropology* 12: 25–69.

Marcus, G. E. and M. M. J. Fischer. 1986. *Anthropology as cultural critique: An experimental moment in the human sciences.* Chicago: University of Chicago Press.

Marcuse, H. 1966. *One-dimensional man: Studies in the ideology of advanced industrial society.* Boston: Beacon Press.

Marling, K. A. 1984. *The colossus of roads: Myth and symbol along the American highway.* Minneapolis: University of Minnesota Press.

Martin, J., M. S. Feldman, M. J. Hatch, and S. Sitkin. 1983. The uniqueness paradox in organizational stories. *Administrative Science Quarterly* 28: 438–53.

Martineau, P. 1958. Social classes and spending behavior. *Journal of Marketing* 23: 121–30.

Marx, L. 1964. *The machine in the garden.* New York: Oxford University Press.

———. 1978. Reflections on the neo-romantic critique of science. *Daedalus* 107: 61–74.

Mead, G. H. 1934. *Mind, self, and society.* Chicago: University of Chicago Press.

Miller, C. R. 1978. Technology as a form of consciousness: A study of contemporary ethos. *Central States Speech Journal* 29: 228–36.

Mintzberg, H. 1973. *The nature of managerial work.* New York: Harper & Row.

Mister, S. M. 1986. Reagan's *Challenger* tribute: Combining generic constraints and situational demands. *Central States Speech Journal* 37: 158–65.

Mitchell, W. J., ed. 1981. *On narrative.* Chicago: University of Chicago Press.

Mitroff, I. I., and R. H. Kilmann 1976. On organizational stories: An approach to the design and analysis of organizations through myths and stories. In *The management of organization design, 1*, ed. R. H. Kilmann, L. R. Pondy, and D. P. Slevin, 189–207. New York: Elsevier-North Holland.

———. 1978. *Methodological approaches to social science.* San Francisco: Jossey-Bass.

Morgan, G. 1983. *Beyond method: Strategies for social research.* Beverly Hills, Calif.: Sage.

———. 1983. More on metaphor: Why we cannot control tropes in administrative science. *Administrative Science Quarterly* 28: 601–7.

———. 1986. *Images of organization.* Beverly Hills, Calif.: Sage.

Morgan, G., P. Frost, and L. Pondy. 1984. Organizational symbolism. In *Organizational symbolism*, ed. L. Pondy et. al. Greenwich, Conn.: JAI.

Morgan, G., and L. Smircich. 1980. The case for qualitative research. *Academy of Management Review* 5: 491–500.

Morris, B. 1977. The culture of technology. *Technology and Culture* 18: 400–410.

Mumford, L. 1934. *Technics and civilization.* New York: Harcourt.

———. 1956. *The highway and the city.* New York: Harcourt.

———. 1961. *The city in history.* New York: Harcourt.

Nash, D., and R. Wintrob. 1972. The emergence of self-consciousness in ethnography. *Current anthropology* 13: 527–42.

Newman, C. 1985. *The post-modern aura: The act of fiction in an age of inflation.* Evanston, Ill.: Northwestern University Press.

Nicol, C. 1987. The hard-boiled go to brunch. *Harper's,* Oct., 61–65.

Nisbet, R. 1976. *Sociology as an art form.* London: Oxford University Press.

Olson, S. R. 1987. Meta-television: Popular postmodernism. *Critical Studies in Mass Communication* 4: 284–300.

Ong, W. J., S.J. 1971. *Rhetoric, romance, and technology.* Ithaca, N.Y.: Cornell University Press.

———. 1977. *Interfaces of the word: Studies in the evolution of consciousness and culture.* Ithaca, N.Y.: Cornell University Press.

———. 1982. *Orality and literacy: The technologizing of the word.* London: Methuen.

Ouchi, W. G., and A. L. Wilkins. 1985. Organizational culture. *Annual Review of Sociology* 11: 457–83.

Outhwaite, W. 1975. *Understanding social life: The method called verstehen.* London: George Allen & Unwin.

Overington, M. A. 1977. The scientific community as audience: Toward a rhetorical analysis of science. *Philosophy and Rhetoric* 10: 151–58.

Pacanowsky, M. E. 1985. Slouching towards Chicago. Paper presented at the Speech Communication Association annual convention, Chicago, November.

Pacanowsky, M. E., and N. O'Donnell-Trujillo. 1982. Communication and organizational cultures. *Western Journal of Speech Communication* 46: 115–30.

———. 1983. Organizational communication as cultural performance. *Communication Monographs* 50: 126–47.

Paretsky, S. 1985. *Deadlock.* New York: William Morrow.

———. 1987. *Bitter medicine.* New York: William Morrow.

Patton, P. 1986. *Open road: A celebration of the American highway.* New York: Simon & Schuster/Touchstone Books.

Percy, W. 1961. *The moviegoer.* New York: Farrar, Straus, Giroux.

———. 1963. *The last gentleman.* New York: Farrar, Straus, Giroux.

———. 1966. *Love in the ruins.* New York: Farrar, Straus, Giroux.

———. 1971. *The message in the bottle.* New York: Farrar, Straus, Giroux.

———. 1975. *Lancelot.* New York: Farrar, Straus, Giroux.

————. 1982. *The second coming.* New York: Farrar, Straus, Giroux.

————. 1985. *Lost in the cosmos.* New York: Farrar, Straus, Giroux.

————. 1987. *The thanatos syndrome.* New York: Farrar, Straus, Giroux.

Persig, R. M. 1974. *Zen and the art of motorcycle maintenance: An inquiry into values.* New York: William Morrow.

Peters, T. J., R. H. Waterman, Jr. 1982. *In search of excellence.* New York: Harper & Row.

Pettey, G. R., R. M. Perloff, K. A. Neuendorf, and B. Pollick. 1986. Feeling and learning about a critical event: The shuttle explodes. *Central States Speech Journal* 36: 166–79.

Pettigrew, A. M. 1979. On studying organizational cultures. *Adminstrative Science Quarterly* 24: 570–81.

Philipsen, G. 1975. Speaking "like a man" in Teamsterville: Cultural patterns of role enactment in an urban neighborhood. *Quarterly Journal of Speech* 61: 13–22.

————. 1977. Linearity of research design in ethnographic studies of speaking. *Communication Quarterly* 25: 42–50.

Phillips, G. M., and H. L. Goodall, Jr. 1983. *Loving and living.* Englewood Cliffs, N.J.: Prentice-Hall/Spectrum Books.

Phillips, G. M., and N. J. Metzger. 1976. *Intimate communication.* Boston: Allyn & Bacon.

Polanyi, M. 1958. *Personal knowledge: Towards a post-critical philosophy.* Chicago: University of Chicago Press.

Pondy, L. R., P. J. Frost, G. Morgan, and T. C. Dandridge, eds. 1983. *Organizational symbolism.* Greenwich, Conn.: JAI.

Potter, S. 1970. *The complete upsmanship.* New York: Holt.

Putnam, L. L. 1982. Paradigms for organizational communication research: An overview and synthesis. *Western Journal of Speech Communication* 46: 192–206.

————. 1984. Contradictions and paradoxes in organizations. In *People, communication, and organizational performance,* ed. L. Thayer and O. Wiio. New York: Ablex.

Putnam, L.L. and G. Cheney. 1984. Organizational communication. In *Speech communication in the twentieth century,* ed. T. W. Benson. Carbondale, Ill: Southern Illinois University Press.

Putnam, L.L., and M. E. Pacanowsky, eds. 1983. *Communication and organizations: An interpretive approach.* Beverly Hills, Calif.. Sage.

Pynchon, T. 1964. *V.* New York: Bantam.

————. 1966. *The crying of lot 49.* New York: Bantam.

————. 1973. *Gravity's rainbow.* New York: Viking.

Rabinow, P. 1986. Representations are social facts: modernity and post-modernity in anthropology. In *Writing culture,* ed. J. Clifford and G. E. Marcus. Berkeley: University of California Press.

Rabinow, P. and W. M. Sullivan, ed. 1979. *Interpretive social science: A reader.* Berkeley: University of California Press.

Radcliffe-Brown, A. R. 1958. The method of ethnology and social anthropology. In *Method in social anthropology,* ed. M. N. Srinivas. Chicago: University of Chicago Press.

Redding, W. C. 1972. *Communication within the organization: An interpretive review of theory and research.* New York: Industrial Communications Council.

————. 1979. Organizational communication theory and ideology: An overview. In *Communication Yearbook 3,* ed. D. Nimmo. New Brunswick, N.J.: ICA/Transaction Books.

Redstone, L. 1973. *New dimensions in shopping centers and stores.* New York: McGraw-Hill.

Riemer, J. 1977. Varieties of opportunistic research. *Urban Life* 5: 467–77.

Riesman, D., and N. Glazer. 1952. *Faces in the crowd.* New Haven, Conn.: Yale University Press.

Riesman, D., N. Glazer, and R. Denney. 1950. *The lonely crowd.* Garden City, N.Y.: Doubleday and Company.

Ritti, R. R., and G. R. Funkhauser. 1977. *The ropes to skip and the ropes to know: Studies in organizational behavior.* Columbus, Ohio: Grid.

Roberts, K. H., and C. A. O'Reilly 1978. Organizations as communication structures. *Human Communication Research* 4: 283–93.

Rogers, E. M. 1962. *Diffusion of innovations.* New York: Free Press.

———. 1982. The empirical and critical schools of communication research. In *Communication Yearbook 5,* ed. M. Burgoon. New Brunswick, N.J.: ICA/Transaction Books.

Rogers, E. M. and L. Kincaid. 1981. *Communication networks.* New York: Free Press.

Rorty, R. 1979. *Philosophy and the Mirror of Nature.* Princeton, N.J.: Princeton University Press.

———. 1983. Postmodernism bourgeois liberalism. *Journal of Philosophy* 80: 583–89.

Rosen, M. 1985. Breakfast at Spiro's: Dramaturgy and dominance. *Journal of management* 11: 31–48.

Rosenfield, L. 1974. The experience of criticism. *Quarterly Journal of Speech* 60: 489–96.

Rowland, R. C. 1986. The relationship between the public and the technical spheres of argument: A case study of the *Challenger* seven disaster. *Central States Speech Journal* 37: 136–46.

Roy, D. F. 1960. "Banana time": Job satisfaction and informal interaction. *Human Organization* 18: 158–68.

Rubin, L. D. 1972. *Worlds of pain: Life in the working-class family.* New York: Basic Books.

Ruby, J., ed. 1982. *A crack in the mirror: Reflexive perspectives in anthropology.* Philadelphia: University of Pennsylvania Press.

Rueckert, W. H. 1982. *Kenneth Burke and the drama of human relations.* 2d. ed. Berkeley: University of California Press.

Runciman, W. G. 1972. *A critique of Max Weber's philosophy of social science.* Cambridge: Cambridge University Press.

Sahlins, M. 1976. *Culture and practical reason.* Chicago: University of Chicago Press.

Sanday, P. R. 1979. The ethnographic paradigms. *Administrative Science Quarterly* 24: 527–38.

Sass, L. A. 1986. Anthropology's native problems. *Harper's,* May.

Sathe, V. 1985. *Culture and related corporate realities.* Homewood, Ill.: Richard D. Irwin.

Savage, C. 1985. *Sons of the machine.* Cambridge, Mass.: M.I.T. Press.

Schall, M. S. 1983. A communication-rules approach to organizational culture. *Administrative Science Quarterly* 28: 557–81.

Schein, E. H. 1985. *Organizational culture and leadership.* San Francisco: Jossey-Bass.

———. 1987. *The clinical perspective in fieldwork.* Beverly Hills, Calif.: Sage.

Scott, R. L. 1967. On viewing rhetoric as epistemic. *Central States Speech Journal* 18: 9–17.

Scott, W., and D. Hart. 1979. *Organizational America.* Boston: Houghton Mifflin.

Seeger, M. W. 1986. The *Challenger* tragedy and search for legitimacy. *Central States Speech Journal* 37: 147–57.

Segal, J. 1985. *Phantasy in everyday life.* Harmondsworth, Eng.: Penguin.

Sennett, R. 1977. *The fall of public man.* New York: Vintage.

———. 1982. *Authority.* New York: Vintage.

Sennett, R., and J. Cobb. 1972. *The hidden injuries of class*. New York: Vintage.

Sheldon, A. 1980. Organizational paradigms: A theory of organizational change. *Organizational Dynamics* 5: 61–80.

Shimanoff, S. B. 1980. *Communication rules theory and research*. Beverly Hills, Calif.: Sage.

Simms, N., ed. 1984. *The literary journalists*. New York: Ballantine.

Simon, H. A. 1957. *Models of man*. New York: Wiley.

―――. 1976. *Administrative behavior* 3d ed. New York: Free Press.

Slack, J. D. 1983. *Communication technologies and society: Conceptions of causality and the politics of technological intervention*. Norwood, N.J.: Ablex.

Slater, P. 1970. *The pursuit of loneliness: American culture at the breaking point*. Boston: Beacon Press.

Smircich, L. 1983. Concepts of culture and organizational analysis. *Administrative Science Quarterly* 28: 339–58.

Smircich, L., and G. Morgan. 1982. Leadership: The management of meaning. *Journal of Applied Behavioral Science* 18: 257–73.

Smircich, L., and C. I. Stubbart. 1985. Strategic management in an enacted world. *Academy of Management Review*. 10: 724–36.

Smith, D. H. 1972. Communication research and the idea of process. *Speech Monographs* 39: 174–82.

Stanley, M. 1978. *The technological conscience: Survival and dignity in an age of expertise*. New York: Free Press.

Stocking, G. W., ed. 1983. *Observers observed*. Madison, Wis.: University of Wisconsin Press.

Stoddart, K. 1985. The presentation of everyday life. *Urban Life* 15: 103–21.

Strine, M. S., and M. E. Pacanowsky. 1985. How to read interpretive accounts of organizational life: Narrative bases of textual authority. *Southern Speech Communication Journal* 50: 283–97.

Sturrock, J., ed. 1979. *Structuralism and since: From Lévi-Straus to Derrida*. New York: Oxford University Press.

Sypher, B. D., J. L. Applegate, and H. E. Sypher. 1985. Culture and communication in organizational contexts. In *Communication, culture, and organizational processes*, ed. W. B. Gudykunst, L. P. Stewart, and S. Ting-Toomey. Beverly Hills, Calif.: Sage.

Tedlock, D. 1983. *The spoken word and the work of interpretation*. Philadelphia: University of Pennsylvania Press.

Tichy, N. M. 1973. An analysis of clique formation and structure in organizations. *Administrative Science Quarterly* 18: 194–208.

Tompkins, P. K. 1977. Management quo communication in rocket research and development. *Communication Monographs* 44: 1–26.

―――. 1978. Organizational metamorphosis in space research and development. *Communication Monographs* 45: 110–18.

―――. 1984. Functions of communication in organizations. In *Handbook of rhetorical and communication theory*, ed. C. Arnold and J. Bowers. Boston: Allyn & Bacon.

―――. 1985. On hegemony—"he gave it no name"—and critical structuralism in the work of Kenneth Burke. *Quarterly Journal of Speech* 71: 119–31.

Tompkins, P. K., J. Fisher, D. Infante, and E. Tompkins. 1975. Kenneth Burke and the inherent characteristics of formal organizations: A field study. *Speech Monographs* 42: 135–42.

Trice, H. M., and J. M. Beyer. 1984. Studying organizational cultures through rites and ceremonials. *Academy of Management Review* 9: 653–69.

Trujillo, N. 1985. Organizational communication as cultural performance: Some managerial considerations. *Southern Speech Communication Journal* 50: 201–24.

Turkel, S. 1984. *The second self: Computers and the human spirit.* New York: Basic Books.

Turner, V. 1974. *Dramas, fields, and metaphors.* Ithaca, N.Y.: Cornell University Press.

———. 1981. Social dramas and stories about them. In *On narrative,* ed. W. J. Mitchell. Chicago: University of Chicago Press.

Tyler, S. A. 1987. *The unspeakable: Discourse, dialogue, and rhetoric in the postmodern world.* Madison: University of Wisconsin Press.

Van Maanen, J. 1973. Observations on the making of policemen. *Human Organization* 32: 407–18.

———. 1979. *Qualitative methods.* Beverly Hills, Calif.: Sage.

———. 1988. *Tales of the field: On writing ethnography.* Chicago: University of Chicago Press.

Van Maanen, J. and S. R. Barley. 1984. Occupational communities: Culture and control in organizations. In *Research in organizational behavior,* ed. B. Staw and L. L. Cummings. Greenwich, Conn.: JAI.

Veblen, T. 1979. *The theory of the leisure class.* New York: Penguin.

Von Wright, G. H. 1971. *Explanation and understanding.* Ithaca, N.Y.: Cornell University Press.

Walster, E., G. W. Walster, and E. Bersheid. 1978. *Equity theory and research.* Boston: Allyn & Bacon.

Wax, M. 1972. Tenting with Malinowski. *American Anthropological Review* 37: 1–13.

Weber, M. 1947. *The theory of social and economic organization.* Trans. T. Parsons. New York: Free Press.

———. 1949. *The methodology of the social sciences.* Glencoe, Ill.: Free Press.

———. 1958. *The Protestant ethic and the spirit of capitalism.* New York: Scribner's.

———. 1968. *Economy and society: An outline of interpretive sociology.* New York: Bedminster.

Weick, K. 1974. Amendments to organizational theorizing. *Academy of Management Journal* 17: 487–502.

———. 1976. Educational organizations as loosely coupled systems. *Administrative Science Quarterly* 21: 1–19.

———. 1979. *The social psychology of organizing.* 2d. ed. Reading, Mass.: Addison-Wesley.

———. 1980. The management of eloquence. *Executive* 6: 18–21.

Weinberg, H. 1959. *Levels of knowing and existence.* New York: Harper & Row.

White, H. 1978. *Tropics of discourse.* Baltimore: Johns Hopkins University Press.

———. 1980. The value of narrativity in the representation of reality. *Critical Inquiry* 7: 5–27.

Whyte, W., Jr. 1951. *The organization man.* New York: Doubleday.

Wilkins, A. L., and W. G. Ouchi. 1983. Efficient cultures: Exploring the relationship between culture and organizational performance. *Administrative Science Quarterly* 28: 468–81.

Wilson, G. L., H. L. Goodall, Jr., and C. L. Waagen. 1986. *Organizational Communication.* New York: Harper & Row.

Winkler, K. J. 1985. Questioning the science in social science, scholars signal a "turn to interpretation." *Chronicle of Higher Education,* 25 June, 5–6.

Winner, L. 1977. *Autonomous technology: Technics-out-of-control as theme in political thought.* Cambridge, Mass.: M.I.T. Press.

———. 1986. *The whale and the reactor: A search for limits in an age of high technology.* Chicago: University of Chicago Press.

Wittgenstein, L. *Philosophical investigations.* Trans. G. E. M. Anscombe. New York: Macmillan.

Wolfe, T., and E. W. Johnson. 1973. *The new journalism.* New York: Ballantine.

Wood, J. T. 1982. *Human communication: A symbolic interaction perspective.* New York: Holt.

———. 1984. Research and the social world: Honoring the real world connections. *Communication Quarterly* 32: 3–8.

Wyatt, N. J., and G. M. Phillips 1988. *Studying organizations: A case history of the Farmer's Home Administration.* Norwood, N.J.: Ablex.

Yankelovich, D. 1981. *The new rules: Searching for self-fulfillment in a world turned upside-down.* New York: Random House.

Yates, F. 1966. *The art of memory.* Chicago: University of Chicago Press.

About the Author

Places: Martinsburg, West Virginia, 8 September 1952. Rome, Paris, London. Cheyenne, Philadelphia, Hagerstown. *Schools:* The American School, St. Dunstan's, Carey Junior, Roxborough, South High, Shepherd College, The University of North Carolina at Chapel Hill, The Pennsylvania State University. *Jobs:* lifeguard, short-order cook, political activist, musician, psychologist's assistant, waiter, account executive, college professor, consultant. *Favorites:* blue, Raymond Chandler, golden retrievers, Italian or Szechwan, Herbert Blumer, Miller Genuine Draft, Bogar's farm. *Current Status:* happily married, gainfully employed.